CAMPAIGN • 254

KHARKOV 1942

The Wehrmacht strikes back

ROBERT FORCZYK

ILLUSTRATED BY HOWARD GERRARD

Series editor Marcus Cowper

First published in Great Britain in 2013 by Osprey Publishing,
PO Box 883, Oxford, OX1 9PL, UK
PO Box 3985, New York, NY 10185-3985, USA
Email: info@ospreypublishing.com

Osprey Publishing, part of Bloomsbury Publishing Plc

Transferred to digital print on demand 2016.

First published 2013
1st impression 2013

Printed and bound in Great Britain

A CIP catalogue record for this book is available from the British
Library.

ISBN: 978 1 78096 157 6
E-pub ISBN: 978 1 78096 159 0
E-book ISBN: 978 1 78096 158 3

Editorial by Ilios Publishing Ltd, Oxford, UK (www.iliospublishing.com)
Index by Angela Hall
Typeset in Myriad Pro and Sabon
Maps by Bounford.com
3D bird's-eye view by The Black Spot
Battlescene illustrations by Howard Gerrard
Originated by PDQ Media, Bungay, UK

Dedication
In remembrance of 1LT Ivan D. Lechowich, 5th Engineer Battalion,
killed by IED attack in Ghazni Province, Afghanistan, 28 September
2011.

Author's note
I wish to thank Nik Cornish, Bill Russ, Ian Barter and Ralph Gibson of
RIA Novosti and the staff of the Bundesarchiv for their help with this
project.

Artist's note
Readers may care to note that the original paintings from which the
color plates in this book were prepared are available for private sale.
The Publishers retain all reproduction copyright whatsoever. All
enquiries should be addressed to:

Howard Gerrard, 11 Oaks Road, Tenterden, Kent, TN30 6RD, UK

The Publishers regret that they can enter into no correspondence
upon this matter.

Glossary
AOK – Armeeoberkommando (Army)
GRD – Guards Rifle Division
GCC – Guards Cavalry Corps
HKL – *Hauptkampflinie* (main line of resistance)
MRL – Multiple Rocket Launcher
OKH – Oberkommando des Heeres
PzAOK – Panzerarmee
TC – Tank Corps

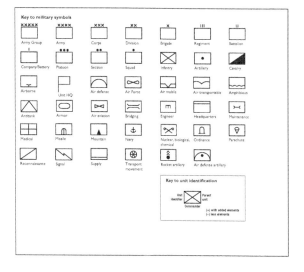

CONTENTS

Creation of the Barvenkovo salient, January–March 1942

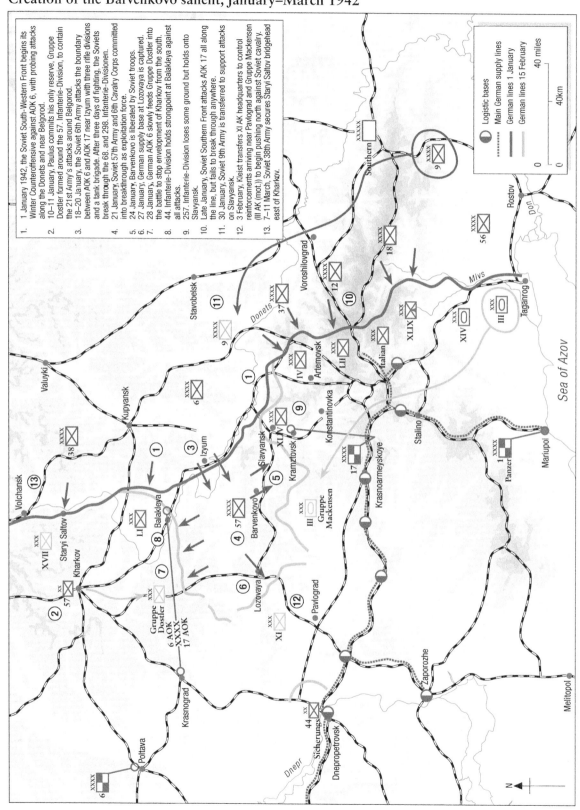

1. 1 January 1942, the Soviet South-Western Front begins its Winter Counteroffensive against AOK 6, with probing attacks along the Donets and near Belgorod.
2. 10–11 January, Paulus commits his only reserve, Gruppe Dostler formed around the 57. Infanterie-Division, to contain the 21st Army's attacks around Belgorod.
3. 18–20 January, the Soviet 6th Army attacks the boundary between AOK 6 and AOK 17 near Izyum with three rifle divisions and a tank brigade. After three days of fighting, the Soviets break through the 68. and 298. Infanterie-Divisionen.
4. 21 January, Soviet 57th Army and 6th Cavalry Corps committed into breakthrough as exploitation force.
5. 24 January, Barvenkovo is liberated by Soviet troops.
6. 27 January, German supply base at Lozovaya is captured.
7. 28 January, German AOK 6 slowly feeds Gruppe Dostler into the battle to stop envelopment of Kharkov from the south.
8. 44. Infanterie-Division holds strongpoint at Balakleya against all attacks.
9. 257. Infanterie-Division loses some ground but holds onto Slavyansk.
10. Late January, Soviet Southern Front attacks AOK 17 all along the line, but fails to break through anywhere.
11. 30 January, Soviet 9th Army is transferred to support attacks on Slavyansk.
12. 3 February, Kleist transfers XI AK headquarters to control reinforcements arriving near Pavlograd and Gruppe Mackensen (III AK (mot.)) to begin pushing north against Soviet cavalry.
13. 7–11 March, Soviet 38th Army secures Staryi Saltov bridgehead east of Kharkov.

Logistic bases

Main German supply lines

German lines 1 January

German lines 15 February

0   40km

0   40 miles

N

ORIGINS OF THE CAMPAIGN

In June 1941, Kharkov was the fourth-largest city in the Soviet Union, with a population of 833,000. Kharkov was also the industrial centre of the Ukraine and an important rail transportation hub. Nevertheless, Hitler's Fuhrer Directive 21, issued on 18 December 1941, paid scant attention to the eastern Ukraine in the guidance provided for the upcoming Operation *Barbarossa* – the invasion of the Soviet Union. Instead, the main objective assigned to Generalfeldmarschall Gerd von Rundstedt's Heeresgruppe Süd in the Ukraine was to destroy all Red Army forces west of the Dnepr River and then capture Kiev. It was assumed that Kharkov and the eastern Ukraine would be easy pickings in subsequent mop-up operations.

Yet, when the invasion began on 22 June 1941, Heeresgruppe Süd spent the entire summer trying to fight its way into Kiev. Rundstedt's advance was spearheaded by Generalfeldmarschall Walter von Reichenau's 6. Armee (AOK 6) and Generaloberst Ewald von Kleist's Panzergruppe 1[1]. The Red Army's South-Western Front under General-Colonel Mikhail Kirponos put up stronger than expected resistance, which caused Hitler to divert Generaloberst Heinz Guderian's Panzergruppe 2 from the advance towards Moscow to instead envelop Kiev from the north. Guderian conducted a classic pincer attack that succeeded in linking up with Kleist's Panzers on 16 September, resulting in the encirclement of much of the South-Western Front in the Kiev pocket. Within ten days, the Germans crushed the pocket, eliminating Kirponos and over 600,000 Soviet troops. After Kiev fell, Hitler directed Heeresgruppe Süd to continue eastwards another 410km to capture the Donets Basin, which he deemed 'important for war industry'. In the vacuum created by the catastrophe at Kiev, the eastern Ukraine seemed ripe for conquest. Rundstedt ordered Kleist to advance upon Rostov and Reichenau to march on Kharkov.

At this point, Marshal Timoshenko took over the remnants of the South-Western Front, which consisted of four understrength armies deployed over a 250km stretch of front between Sumy and Dnepropetrovsk. He established a new defensive line west of Kharkov with the 38th Army in early October, just as AOK 6 was gathering around Poltava. Reichenau's advance towards Kharkov was hindered by periods of snow, sleet and mud that reduced the Ukrainian roads to the consistency of oatmeal. Furthermore, German logistics were near collapse, which deprived Heeresgruppe Süd of the resources for all-out attacks. On the other side, Timoshenko was forced

---

1   Renamed Panzerarmee 1 (PzAOK 1) on 25 October 1941.

to rely upon 'instant divisions' created with little or no training and negligible artillery and tank support. Since the Stavka was concentrating all available resources to stop Operation *Typhoon*'s advance on Moscow, Timoshenko could expect no significant external help for the time being. Furthermore, Kleist's panzers surrounded two-thirds of the Southern Front's forces along the Sea of Azov on 6–11 October, threatening Timoshenko's left flank.

Despite bad weather and logistical problems, Timoshenko could not stop Reichenau's AOK 6, which fought its way into Kharkov on 24 October. Within a matter of days, the Donbas region east of the city was occupied by AOK 17 and Kleist's Panzers. Although Hitler directed Kleist to continue his advance towards Rostov, AOK 6 had accomplished all its objectives by late October 1941 and Reichenau positioned his tired infantry in a defensive line east of Kharkov along the Northern Donets River. His main concern was the tenuous situation on his left flank, with only a loose connection with Heeresgruppe Mitte's AOK 2. Meanwhile, Kleist succeeded in capturing Rostov but his forces were too over-extended and he could not hold onto it; by early December Panzergruppe 1 and AOK 17 were consolidating a defensive line behind the Mius River and Donbas region, while AOK 6 anchored the line at Kharkov. As a result of the setback at Rostov, Hitler relieved Rundstedt and put Reichenau in command of Heeresgruppe Süd, while the untried Paulus was given command of AOK 6.

After the German defeat at Moscow and Kleist's retreat from Rostov, the Stavka pressured Timoshenko to re-capture Kharkov. By the beginning of 1942, the South-Western Front had the 40th, 21st, 38th and 6th Armies deployed in an arc from north to south, 40km east of Kharkov. Timoshenko ambitiously planned to conduct a double envelopment of Kharkov, with the 40th and 21st Armies crossing the Northern Donets, seizing Belgorod and then swinging in from the north, while the 38th and 6th Armies crossed the Northern Donets near Izyum then swung in from the south.

Armeeoberkommando 6 had been reduced to nine infantry divisions, strung out along a 245km front and Paulus only had General der Infanterie Anton Dostler's[2] 57. Infanterie-Division in reserve. On 1 January 1942, Timoshenko began his offensive with all four armies attacking. The weather was horrendous, with temperatures of -20°F and deep snow, which made operations extremely difficult. Early on, the northern pincer ran into trouble and Paulus committed part of Gruppe Dostler to blunt the 21st Army's attack near Belgorod. Reduced to only one pincer, Timoshenko continued to pound away at the junction between AOK 6's right flank and AOK 17's left flank near Izyum. For two weeks, Soviet infantry attacked XXXXIV Armeekorps (AK), which held this critical sector. On 18 January, the Soviet 6th Army stepped up its attacks, committing three rifle divisions and a tank brigade. After three days of fighting, the German 298. Infanterie-Division finally crumbled and broke, enabling Timoshenko's infantry to penetrate the German front and cross the Northern Donets on both sides of Izyum. Amidst this crisis, Reichenau suddenly died of a stroke and Bock was brought in to command Heeresgruppe Süd. Bock arrived to find a discouraging situation: a great hole had been torn in the German front and Heeresgruppe Süd lacked any kind of reserves to plug it. Timoshenko quickly committed several of his cavalry divisions into the breach, pursuing the defeated XXXXIV AK and pushing southwards into the 40km-wide gap between AOK 6 and AOK 17. The only bright spot for Bock was that German forces continued to hold key positions on the shoulders of the penetration – the 44. Infanterie-Division at Balakleya and the 257. Infanterie-Division at Slavyansk – which prevented Timoshenko from further widening his penetration corridor.

For the next two months, Bock, Paulus and Kleist were forced to fight a desperate battle to contain the Soviet breakthrough. Initially, Bock had nothing except the disorganized remnants of the 298. Infanterie-Division and some construction battalions to try and plug the gap, but he directed Kleist's 1. Panzerarmee (PzAOK 1) to transfer General der Infanterie Joachim von Kortzfleisch's XI AK headquarters to take command over reinforcements that were en route to rebuild the front between AOK 6 and AOK 17. In desperation, Bock combed his rear area security forces and gave Kortzfleisch the 1st Romanian Division and the 454. Sicherungs-Division to hold onto Pavlograd and Krasnograd. Kleist assumed responsibility for holding the line at Slavyansk and took control over part of AOK 17 as well, so his command was dubbed 'Armee-Gruppe von Kleist'. Meanwhile, Timoshenko's success at Izyum stood in stark contrast to failed attacks on other fronts and the Stavka provided him with the 57th Army, part of the Southern Front's 9th Army and three rebuilt cavalry corps as reinforcements to expand his breakthrough. With these reinforcements, Timoshenko's offensive made rapid progress, with 57th Army liberating Barvenkovo on 24 January and 6th Army advancing 60km to occupy an important German supply base at Lozovaya on 27 January. He then released the 1st and 5th Cavalry Corps to advance south towards the Dnepr River, while 6th Cavalry Corps pushed towards Krasnograd. Timoshenko's creation of the Barvenkovo salient threatened to split Heeresgruppe Süd apart and Kortzfleisch's anaemic corps was unable to stop the Soviet cavalry. From the beginning, Bock knew that the only real solution to this crisis was to cut off the Barvenkovo salient

---

2   Dostler was later executed by the US Army for alleged war crimes in December 1945.

with a pincer attack from Paulus' AOK 6 and Armee-Gruppe von Kleist, but this proved logistically impossible in late January. By early February, Paulus committed the remainder of Gruppe Dostler on the northern edge of the Soviet salient while Kleist formed Stossgruppe Hube with 16. Panzer-Division on the southern flank. Amidst heavy snow storms, Kleist attacked northwards into the flank of 57th Army and managed to recover some ground. However, Paulus dawdled with his part of the counterattack until 8 February and Bock berated him, saying that 'I can't allow forces as strong as Gruppe Dostler to sit there uselessly while other sectors of the front are ablaze.'

Although the Stavka provided Timoshenko with four more rifle brigades and 315 tanks in early February, he diverted most of these fresh troops to capture Slavyansk rather than pressing on to the Dnepr. Despite repeated attacks, Kleist's defence of that town held and the best Red Army units were worn down in futile frontal attacks. By mid-February, it was clear that Timoshenko's forces were nearly spent and Bock was finally able to establish a very thin defence around the Barvenkovo salient. Even XI AK, reinforced by the 113. Infanterie-Division, the Romanian 2nd Infantry Division and an excellent Romanian ski battalion, was ordered to counterattack and managed to retake some ground. However, Timoshenko had noted the appearance of Romanian troops on the front line and he concentrated four tank brigades against the Romanian 1st Infantry Division on 20 February. Lacking adequate anti-tank weaponry, the Romanian division was 'torn to shreds' by the Soviet tanks, suffering nearly 3,000 casualties, and the tenuous connection between AOK 6 and Armee-Gruppe von Kleist broken again. Soviet armour hit the Romanians a week later and the result was the same, but this time the Soviet breakthrough overran two German artillery battalions. Eventually, Kleist was able to restore the front by early March and the Soviet forces in the Barvenkovo paused as the spring thaw approach.

By November 1941, AOK 6 had accomplished its primary mission and its troops had shifted to a defensive posture. However, once the winter weather arrived, most troops were concentrated in *Stützpunkte* (strongpoints) built inside villages. (Ian Barter)

Just before the thaw, Timoshenko made another try to get across the Northern Donets north-east of Kharkov and this time he succeeded. Moskalenko's 38th Army was able to get three reinforced regiments across the Northern Donets near Staryi Saltov on 7–8 March and seize a small bridgehead. Timoshenko committed a tank battalion into the bridgehead, including some KV-1 heavy tanks. Although Bock had been husbanding the 3. Panzer-Division in Kharkov for eventual use against the Barvenkovo salient, he was forced to commit a sizeable *Kampfgruppe*[3] from it to seal off the Staryi Saltov breach. Rapid German counterattacks limited Moskalenko to a 9km-deep bridgehead on the western side of the Northern Donets and inflicted over 2,500 casualties on the 38th Army. Although Moskalenko had gained a useful bridgehead for later operations, Timoshenko failed to note three dangerous trends revealed by the Staryi Saltov attack: the German response was swift, Soviet losses were heavy and Soviet forces could not achieve a decisive penetration of German defences. Afterwards, less intense fighting continued around Staryi Saltov and the Barvenkovo salient throughout March–April, but the spring thaw soon imposed an operational pause upon both sides.

From the Stavka perspective, Timoshenko's South-Western Front had achieved a partial success, at the acceptable cost of about 40,000 casualties. German defences around Kharkov had held – but just barely – and Timoshenko's bridgeheads across the Northern Donets represented a golden opportunity to encircle AOK 6 and thereby gain the initiative in the eastern Ukraine. The Stavka began considering plans for another major offensive at Kharkov in the spring. From the OKH perspective, the Soviet Winter Counteroffensive had been a painful nightmare, but it had fallen short of decisive results and left some of the Red Army's best forces in the vulnerable Barvenkovo salient. Although difficulties with moving reinforcements up by rail and constant Soviet attacks upon AOK 6 had prevented a timely German counterattack against the Barvenkovo salient earlier, Bock viewed the spring thaw as a pause that would give him time to gather his forces for the long-awaited riposte to Timoshenko' breakthrough. Thus both sides hunkered down during the spring rains around Kharkov, replacing losses and regrouping. When the weather cleared, both the Red Army and the Wehrmacht intended to launch a major offensive that would decide the issue at Kharkov.

---

3   Kampfgruppe Beaulieu included Schützen-Regiment 394, Kradschützen-Bataillon 3 and a Panzer company with 12 P/PzKpw III tanks.

CHRONOLOGY

1941

21 August	Hitler assigns Heeresgruppe Süd the mission of capturing Kharkov and the Donbas region.
24 October	AOK 6 captures Kharkov.

1942

1 January	Timoshenko launches South-Western Front Winter Counteroffensive, intended to recapture Kharkov.
24 January	Barvenkovo liberated.
31 January	Heeresgruppe Süd contains Timoshenko's offensive.
7–11 March	Moskalenko's 38th Army gains a bridgehead across the Northern Donets at Staryi Saltov.
25 March	Heeresgruppe Süd issues preliminary warning order for Operation *Fridericus*.
27–30 March	Timoshenko submits proposal to Stavka to conduct a pincer offensive against German AOK 6 around Kharkov.
10 April	Stalin approves Timoshenko's revised offensive plan.
8 May	Operation *Trappenjagd* begins in the Crimea.
12 May	Soviet South-Western Front offensive begins. 38th Army captures Nepokrytaya. Army Group Bobkin achieves successful breakthrough.
13 May	The 28th Army captures Peremoga and encircles Gruppe Grüner in Ternovaya. German 3. and 23. Panzer-Divisionen successfully counterattack 38th Army.
14 May	Fliegerkorps IV gains air superiority over Kharkov sector. Soviet 21st Army encircles Murom. Heavy fighting around Efremovka.

15 May	Counterattack by 3. Panzer-Division shatters front of 28th Army. VIII Armeekorps falls back behind Berestovaia River.
16 May	6th Cavalry Corps surrounds IR 576 in Krasnograd.
17 May	Panzergruppe Kleist begins Operation *Fridericus* to cut off the Barvenkovo salient, routing the Soviet 9th Army. The Soviet 21st and 23rd Tank Corps are finally committed to exploit 6th Army's success. The 3. Panzer-Division relieves Gruppe Grüner in Ternovaya.
18 May	Kleist's Panzers reach southern part of Izyum.
19 May	Counterattack by Kampfgruppe Gollwitzer reaches Murom and forces 21st Army to retreat. Timoshenko forms Army Group Kostenko inside Barvenkovo salient.
20 May	Timoshenko suspends offensive by northern group. AOK 6 begins reorienting forces to assist in battle of Barvenkovo salient.
21 May	Group Sherstiuk formed outside salient as relief force.
22 May	Kleist's Panzers link-up with LI Armeekorps, cutting off Army Group Kostenko in Barvenkovo salient.
23 May	German 3. and 23. Panzer-Divisionen begin attacking northern side of Barvenkovo pocket.
24 May	German VIII Armeekorps and Romanian 6th Corps join attack on Barvenkovo pocket.
24–27 May	Repeated efforts by Army Group Kostenko to fights its way out of the pocket fail.
28 May	Organized resistance in the Barvenkovo pocket ends. Timoshenko orders South-Western Front onto defensive.
10–15 June	AOK 6 conducts Operation *Wilhelm*, eliminating the Staryi Saltov bridgehead.
22–25 June	Kleist conducts *Fridericus II*, pushing back left flank of South-Western Front.
28 June	Heeresgruppe Süd begins main summer offensive, Operation *Blau*.

OPPOSING COMMANDERS

GERMAN COMMANDERS

Generalfeldmarschall Fedor von Bock (1880–1945), commander of Heeresgruppe Süd from 20 January 1942. Bock was born into a Prussian military family that combined rigid Lutheran thinking with intense German nationalism, in order to mould him into an obedient soldier. He then was given a narrow military education at the Gross Lichterfelde Military Academy in Potsdam, followed by a commission as an infantry officer in 1898. Bock was not particularly intelligent, but he was fashionable and aristocratic, which enabled him to use his social and professional relationships to facilitate his career ambitions. During World War I, Bock served as a company-grade officer on the Western Front and rose to battalion command by early 1916. After the war, he was retained in the Reichswehr and managed to rise rapidly, commanding infantry units from battalion up to corps in the interwar period. Despite his aristocratic connections, Bock's career continued to prosper when Hitler came to power, primarily because of his willingness to be used as a tool of aggression; he commanded the German forces involved in the Austrian Anschluss in 1938, then the occupation of Czechoslovakia in 1938–39, then Heeresgruppe Nord during the invasion of Poland in September 1939.

By the spring of 1940, Bock was one of the most prominent generals in the Wehrmacht and he was given command of Heeresgruppe B, which was tasked to invade Holland and Belgium. After the quick victory in the West, Bock's formation was redesignated Heeresgruppe Mitte and transferred to Poland for the upcoming invasion of the Soviet Union in June 1941. By this point, Hitler regarded Bock as solid and reliable, so he entrusted him with the main effort in Operation *Barbarossa*. In Russia, Bock kept pushing for a drive straight on Moscow and openly criticized Hitler's decision to divert his armour to crush the Soviet South-Western Front in the Kiev pocket. Bock's Heeresgruppe Mitte was finally redirected towards Moscow with Operation *Typhoon* in October 1941, but failed just short of objective. When the Soviet Winter Counteroffensive began to push back Heeresgruppe Mitte in disorder, Hitler decided that Bock needed a rest and relieved him on 18 December 1941. However, Hitler still had great confidence in Bock and brought him out of Führer Reserve just one month later to command Heeresgruppe Süd after the sudden death of Generalfeldmarschall Walter von Reichenau. Bock first had to contain the Soviet breakthrough at Izyum and then rebuild Heeresgruppe Süd in order to be the main effort for the German summer

Generalfeldmarschall Fedor von Bock, commander of Heeresgruppe Süd. (Author)

1942 offensive. Bock was a capable military professional but his methodical and humourless methods prevented him from being a charismatic leader. During the Kharkov campaign, Bock was at the top of his game and was able to quickly assess battlefield conditions and make rapid decisions.

General der Panzertruppen Friedrich Paulus (1890–1957), commander of AOK 6 from 30 December 1941. Unlike most other senior Wehrmacht commanders, Friedrich Paulus came from a non-military Prussian family and had not sought a military career. However, after failing to become a lawyer, Paulus opted to join the German army in 1910. During World War I, he saw action in France as a junior infantry officer, but then spent much of the war as a staff officer in the elite Alpenkorps, serving in Italy, Serbia and at Verdun. During the interwar period, Paulus made a reputation as a diligent and skilled staff officer in the Reichswehr. However, other than 18 months as a peacetime infantry battalion commander, he had negligible command experience. In 1935, Paulus got another lucky break by being assigned as chief of staff to Generalleutnant Oswald Lutz's Panzer command, and three years later he became Heinz Guderian's chief of staff. At the start of World War II, Paulus served as a staff officer in the Polish and Western campaigns. After the fall of France, Paulus was promoted to *Generalleutnant* and made deputy chief of the General Staff. His primary responsibility in the winter of 1940/41 became drafting the logistic plans for Operation *Barbarossa*.

General der Panzertruppen Friedrich Paulus, commander AOK 6. Paulus' performance at Kharkov revealed some of his weaknesses as a commander, which concerned Bock. (Bundesarchiv, Bild 183-B24575)

Once *Barbarossa* began in June 1941, Paulus sat out the first six months of the campaign in Berlin, which kept him removed from realities of combat in Russia. It was not until Reichenau was moved from AOK 6 to take over Heeresgruppe Süd in December that Paulus was sent out to the Eastern Front. Despite lack of command experience with Panzer units, he was promoted to *General der Panzertruppen* and given command of AOK 6. Paulus was considered an expert in logistical planning, but his proper place was in the OKH, not field command. It is almost inconceivable that the German Army, which characteristically put such care into selecting and training field commanders, would place an officer with no division or corps command experience in charge of an important army. During the Kharkov campaign, Paulus began to demonstrate that he was ill suited for higher command, particularly during a crisis. Bock judged him to be indecisive and slow to act, as well as demonstrating little concern for his troops.

Generaloberst Ewald von Kleist (1881–1954), commander of Panzergruppe 1 (later renamed 1. Panzerarmee) since June 1941. Kleist came from an aristocratic family in Hesse and was originally commissioned as an artillery officer in the Prussian Army in 1904. However, Kleist served most of World War I in cavalry units on both Eastern and Western fronts, including a mix of staff and command assignments. After the war, he commanded an infantry regiment, then the 2. Kavallerie-Division, but he did not fare as well under the Nazis as Bock. In February 1938, General der Kavallerie von Kleist was forced into retirement after his opposition to the Fritsch affair. At the outbreak of World War II, Kleist was reinstated and played a minor role in the Polish Campaign. Nevertheless, he was given the star role in the 1940 Western Campaign, leading Panzergruppe von Kleist in the *Sichelschnitt* to the Channel Coast. In April 1941, Kleist's command was redesignated Panzergruppe 1 and he led it in the conquest of Yugoslavia and Greece, as well as the invasion of the Soviet Union in June 1941. Kleist's Panzers cut across the Ukraine and helped to encircle the bulk of the Soviet

Generaloberst Ewald von Kleist, commander of Panzerarmee 1. Kleist was one of the most experienced and aggressive Panzer leaders in the Wehrmacht. (Bundesarchiv, Bild 183-1986-0210-503)

South-Western Front in the Kiev pocket in September 1941 and then much of the Southern Front in October. Unlike many of his peers, Kleist retained his command during the winter of 1941/42 and succeeded in withdrawing from Rostov without being relieved by Hitler. By the time of the battle of Kharkov, Kleist was one of the most experienced leaders of large Panzer formations in the Wehrmacht and thoroughly skilled in manoeuvre warfare. Kleist was an aggressive leader and Bock noted that he was always ready to attack.

Generaloberst Eberhard von Mackensen (1889–1969), commander of III Armeekorps (mot.) from February 1941. Son of Generalfeldmarschall August von Mackensen, Eberhard was commissioned as a cavalry officer in 1908. He served primarily as a staff officer in World War I, the interwar period and the opening campaigns of the start of World War II. Despite his illustrious military heritage, Mackensen had negligible large-formation command experience prior to Operation *Barbarossa* and was not unlike Paulus. Nevertheless, Mackensen demonstrated great timing and troop handling ability during the Kharkov campaign, making the most of his available forces.

SOVIET COMMANDERS

Marshal Semyon K. Timoshenko (1895–1970), commander of the South-Western Front from September 1941. Timoshenko was a professional cavalry officer who had forged close ties with Stalin and Semyon Budyonny in the 1st Cavalry Army (Konarmia) during the Russian Civil War. He thrived in the interwar period, using his political connections to avoid the purges of 1937–40 and succeeding in becoming People's Commissar of Defence in 1940. However, Timoshenko had limited grasp of modern military technology and had no head for strategic or operational-level planning, so he tended to rely upon talented subordinates such as Georgy Zhukov. He did enjoy Stalin's confidence and was sent to pick up the pieces after the initial Soviet defeats in the Russo-Finnish War in 1939–40. With the help of Kirill Meretskov, who could plan a set-piece battle, Timoshenko's forces were eventually able to batter their way through the Mannerheim Line, which earned him the award of Hero of the Soviet Union. Afterwards, Timoshenko spent the next year trying to prepare the Red Army for war, including rapid efforts to strengthen mechanized forces. When the German invasion began in June 1941, Timoshenko was chairman of the Stavka and Stalin sent him to take over the Western Front in July. Timoshenko conducted a dogged but ultimately unsuccessful defence of Smolensk, with most of his command surrounded and destroyed. After Smolensk, Stalin sent Timoshenko to take over what was left of the shattered South-Western Front after the disastrous Kiev encirclement. Timoshenko lost Kharkov and the Donets basin, but was gradually able to stabilize the situation by late 1941 and then launched a partially successful counteroffensive in January 1942. Although Timoshenko had an impressive martial bearing, he proved poorly suited as a front commander since he lacked the skill to oversee a complex operation and was plagued by indecisiveness.

General-Major Kirill S. Moskalenko (1902–85), commander of the 38th Army from March 1942. Moskalenko was born in a peasant family in south-east Ukraine and was drafted into the Red Army in August 1920.

Marshal Semyon K. Timoshenko, commander of the South-Western Front. Timoshenko tried to fight a set-piece battle at Kharkov, trusting in superior numbers and firepower. Yet he failed to appreciate the effects of German air supremacy and manoeuvre warfare on the battlefield. (RIA Novosti, 7263)

Since he had received some schooling, he was sent to an artillery course in Kharkov and then commissioned as an artillery officer. Moskalenko enjoyed a 'lucky' career, beginning with service in Budyonny's 1st Cavalry Army in the Russian Civil War. Afterwards, he spent virtually the entire interwar period in cavalry units and managed to survive the Stalinist purges, but then transitioned to mechanized units in 1935. During the Russo-Finnish War, Moskalenko commanded the artillery regiment of a rifle division and managed to enhance his reputation with an Order of Lenin. In recognition of his abilities, Moskalenko was given command of the 1st Anti-Tank Brigade in the Kiev Military District in May 1941. In this capacity, Moskalenko was tasked with stopping the initial attacks of Kleist's Panzergruppe 1 across the border. Although Moskalenko's brigade was gradually destroyed, his contribution to slowing the German drive on Kiev was noteworthy. He was again fortunate in escaping the Kiev encirclement. In January 1942, Timoshenko put him in command of the 6th Cavalry Corps for the counteroffensive south of Kharkov that led to the creation of the Barvenkovo Salient. Moskalenko was about as capable a field commander as the Red Army could find in early 1942, although his command experience with large formations was limited and he had negligible experience in planning a large-scale attack. During the Kharkov operation, Timoshenko consistently ignored Moskalenko's sound recommendations. After Kharkov, Moskalenko continued his lucky career and was eventually made a Marshal of the Soviet Union in 1955.

General-Colonel Aleksandr M. Vasilevsky (1895–1977), chief of the General Staff and Stavka representative to the South-Western Front. Vasilevsky was one of the most talented operational planners in the Red Army and played a major role in planning all major Soviet counteroffensives from 1941 onwards. Oddly, he was the son of a priest and intent on becoming a teacher. In 1915 he volunteered to join the Tsarist Army and saw considerable combat as a company commander in the Brusilov Offensive. Once the Tsarist regime collapsed, Vasilevsky tried to revert to civilian life but was drafted into the Red Army and saw further combat service in both the Russian Civil War and the Russo-Polish War. During the interwar period, Vasilevsky was marked as an up-and-coming staff officer and assigned to the Directorate of Training in 1931. Six years later, Vasilevsky received General Staff training and soon moved into the operations directorate. At the start of the war, Vasilevsky soon became deputy chief of the General Staff and he played a major role in planning the Moscow Counteroffensive. Vasilevsky's planning skills were critical for completing the detailed planning for the Kharkov offensive, but he was only an advisor to Timoshenko during the actual conduct of operations. Vasilevsky instinctively knew that the Kharkov offensive was a high-risk venture, but lacked the moral courage to make this case to Stalin until it was too late.

General-Lieutenant Dmitri I. Ryabyshev (1894–1985), commander 28th Army from 8 May 1942. Ryabyshev came from a Cossack family near Rostov and after a brief stint in the Tsarist Army in World War I, he joined the Red Army in October 1917. He joined the Konarmia during the Russian Civil War and rose rapidly, from platoon leader to division commander. After the Civil War, he received formal military training at the Frunze Military Academy in Moscow but spent the bulk of the interwar period in command of various cavalry units. In June 1940, Ryabyshev was given command of the 8th Mechanized Corps in the Kiev Military District and he

General-Lieutenant Dmitri I. Ryabyshev, commander 28th Army. Ryabyshev was an old-style Russian cavalryman, unfamiliar with tanks or combined arms warfare. (Author)

General-Lieutenant Avksentiy M. Gorodniansky, commander 6th Army. Despite the lack of much higher level command experience, Gorodniansky was given one of the most important assignments of the Soviet offensive. (Author)

played a major role in the initial tank battles around Lutsk and Brody in June 1941. However, his corps was quickly reduced to fragments and he was given command of the 38th Army and then, briefly, the Southern Front in September 1941. During autumn 1941, the Stavka tasked him with forming the 57th Army, which was then used by Timoshenko to spearhead his offensive that created the Barvenkovo salient in January 1942. Ryabyshev was a parochial cavalry officer, with limited command potential beyond corps-level; he was ill suited to command an army.

General-Lieutenant Avksentiy M. Gorodniansky (1896–1942), commander 6th Army from January 1942. Gorodniansky was drafted into the Tsarist Army and became an NCO during World War I. Afterwards, he joined the Red Army in 1918, served in the Russian Civil War and was commissioned as an infantry officer. At the start of the German invasion in June 1941, Gorodniansky was in command of the 129th Rifle Division and fought under Timoshenko in the battle of Smolensk. Later in the year, he was given command of the 13th Army and successfully led it in counterattacks against the German AOK 2 near Yelets. Like most Soviet commanders in 1942, Gorodniansky was best suited to set-piece battles rather than fluid battles of manoeuvre.

General-Major Leonid V. Bobkin (1894–1942), commander Bobkin Operational Group and deputy commander South-Western Front. Like many senior Soviet commanders, Bobkin was a cavalry officer and veteran of both World War I and the Russian Civil War. In the wake of the Stalinist purges of 1937, Bobkin rose quickly from brigade commander to corps commander in little more than a year. At the start of the war, he was commander of cavalry in the South-Western Front and fought at Kiev and then in the South-Western Front's Winter Counteroffensive in January 1942.

OPPOSING FORCES

GERMAN

Infantry

On average, the infantry divisions in AOK 6 were each holding about 18km of front line at the start of the Kharkov campaign. However, some units were assigned even larger sectors, such as 62. Infanterie-Division, which held 31km of front. According to German defensive doctrine, a full-strength infantry division could defend an 8–10km-wide front, preferably with at least one battalion in reserve. However, after nearly a year of combat, many of the German infantry divisions had been reduced to about two-thirds of authorized troop strength. For example, the three infantry regiments in the 79. Infanterie-Division ranged from 58 per cent strength in IR 429 to 72 per cent strength in IR 212. Nor was the German Ersatzheer (Replacement Army) able to replace losses effectively; the 79. Infanterie-Division suffered over 1,400 casualties in March–April 1942 but received only 1,000 replacements, of which just five were officers. Consequently, Paulus' AOK 6 lacked sufficient troops or weapons to hold its front in any strength, which invited attack. Instead, German units opted for *Stützpunkt* (strongpoint) defences based upon fortified villages during the winter battles and they

Paulus was forced to use security troops from the 454. Sicherungs-Division to hold a significant section of the front line surrounding the Barvenkovo salient. The security troops were mainly equipped with older weapons, like the MP28 machine pistol (centre) and the Czech-made MG 26(t) 7.92mm light machine gun (left). (Nik Cornish at Stavka)

continued this tactic in the spring as well. By concentrating a battalion-size force in a village surrounded by trenches, barbed wire and some mines, relatively small forces could control key terrain, but often at the cost of being surrounded by Soviet infantry.

One oddity in the German front line was the inclusion of the 454. Sicherungs-Division in XI AK's sector. This division had been involved in anti-partisan operations in the Ukraine since the invasion began and was not prepared for front-line combat duty when it was committed on 7 February 1942. It was still in the front line at the start of the Soviet offensive and it had a mixed bag of six security battalions and only one artillery battalion but lacked the *Panzerjäger* battalion normally organic to an infantry division.

Anti-tank capabilities

The German Army had received quite a shock when it encountered the Soviet KV-1 and T-34 tanks in June 1941 and discovered that its 3.7cm and 5cm anti-tank guns were virtually useless against them. Eleven months later, the German anti-tank situation had not improved much and the first 7.5cm anti-tank guns were not expected to arrive in quantity until June. For *Fridericus*, AOK 6 still had to rely upon its own divisional artillery and Luftwaffe 8.8cm Flak guns to stop Soviet heavy tanks. The Stielgranate 41 hollow charge round for the 3.7cm Pak gun was available in small quantities (ranging from ten to 100 per division), but it had poor capabilities against moving targets. In order to prevent some of the 'tank panic' that had occurred in 1941, AOK 6 began providing special training in close combat against enemy tanks to select infantry units in April.

In May 1942, the average infantry division in Heeresgruppe Süd had 20–30 3.7cm Pak and ten 5cm Pak, although the 44. Infanterie-Division defending Balakleya was reinforced and had 62 3.7cm and five 5cm Pak guns. A few divisions, such as the 3. Panzer-Division, were provided with 12 captured Soviet 7.62cm guns, which were quite effective but suffered from limited ammunition supply. In order to deal with Soviet heavy tanks, Generalmajor Hans-Valentin Hube's 16. Panzer-Division was given a battery of four 10cm s.K18 canons, equipped with 1,200 rounds of 10cm Pzgr. rot, which could destroy KV-1 tanks at ranges of 1,000–1,500m. However, the final line of anti-tank defence typically consisted of Luftwaffe 8.8cm Flak guns in the ground role; these large weapons were vulnerable once spotted, but could destroy any Soviet tanks.

Panzer divisions

The cutting edge of German offensive power in the Kharkov campaign was provided by four Panzer divisions (3, 14, 16, 23), which had a total of 421 tanks in 11 Panzer battalions. Each division also had a battalion of infantry mounted in SPW half-tracks and two to three more infantry battalions mounted in tucks. Panzer divisions fought as combined arms *Kampfgruppen*, usually with tanks, infantry, engineers, *Panzerjäger*, artillery and Flak, which provided even relatively small assault groups with a very deadly combat synergy. For example, Kampfgruppe Schmidt-Ott from 3. Panzer-Division consisted of the Stabskompanie/Panzer-Regiment 6, Major Ziervogel's III/Pz.Rgt. 6 with 50 tanks, a *Panzergrenadier* battalion mounted in SPW half-tracks, a motorized pioneer company and a towed battery of 10.5cm l.FH18 howitzers. German tactical skill, particularly in the Panzer units, was at its apogee and often made up for inferior numbers or equipment.

By early May 1942, most of Heeresgruppe Süd's Panzer divisions were back up to about 50–60 per cent of their authorized strength, although the newly-raised 23. Panzer-Division was at full establishment. This Panzer division had been formed in France in late 1941 and did not reach the Eastern Front until mid-April, just weeks before the Kharkov campaign began. Among the four Panzer divisions, the medium PzKpfw III now comprised two-thirds of the available tanks and the PzKpfw IV comprised 20 per cent. About 112 long-barrelled PzKpfw III Ausf. J/1 tanks armed with the 5cm KwK 39 L/60 cannon and 17 PzKpfw IV Ausf. F2 armed with the 7.5cm KwK 40 L/43 cannon had reached Heeresgruppe Süd prior to the Soviet offensive and these improved models could meet the Soviet T-34 tank on relatively even terms. While the bulk of the short-barrelled PzKpfw III and PzKpfw IV tanks were inferior to the Soviet T-34s and KV-1 tanks, the introduction of the 7.5cm Gr. 38 Hl hollow-charge round provided a limited ability to immobilize, if not destroy, their better-armed opponents. In addition, AOK 6 had Sturmgeschütz-Abteilung 244 and Kleist had Sturmgeschütz-Abteilung 245, each with about 20 short-barrelled StuG III assault guns. The StuG III at this point had a limited anti-tank capability, also based upon the 7.5cm Gr. 38 Hl hollow charge round. The 60. Infanterie-Division (mot.) had an attached *Panzerjäger* company with 14 Marder II 7.62cm self-propelled tank destroyers that were among the most effective counters to the T-34.

Heeresgruppe Süd also began to receive a few of the upgraded PzKpfw IVF2 tank during spring 1942. Here, one of the 23. Panzer-Division's newly arrived PzKpfw IVF2 tanks is being camouflaged with brush next to an izba. (Author)

Luftwaffe close air support

By spring 1942, Luftwaffe air support in Russia was becoming an all or nothing proposition – with only ground units designated as main effort receiving support – but it was still used in concentrated fashion to produce operational results. In early May 1942, the bulk of the Luftwaffe's strength in the Ukraine was supporting Manstein's offensive against the Kerch Peninsula in the Crimea, leaving Fliegerkorps IV with only modest forces to protect the airspace around Kharkov. At the start of Timoshenko's offensive, there were only seven Bf-109Fs belonging to III/JG 77 based at Kharkov; this veteran group had just returned from six weeks' rest in Austria and was fully refreshed and re-equipped. For battlefield interdiction, Fliegerkorps IV initially relied upon III/KG 27 and II/KG 55, which had a total of 60 He-111H bombers. All of the Ju-87 Stuka and Hs-129 ground attack aircraft were supporting Manstein when the Soviet offensive at Kharkov began, which meant that Luftwaffe close air support capabilities were negligible at the start of the campaign.

However, once squadrons began returning from the Crimea, Luftwaffe close air support capabilities proved decisive. The German Bf-109F fighter squadrons were vastly superior to their Soviet opponents at this point and, once they gained air superiority over an area, the 100 Ju-87 Stukas from StG 77 would arrive en masse to pulverize Soviet units caught on open terrain. Timoshenko had also underestimated German battlefield interdiction capabilities against the Soviet bridges over the Donets, and the He-111 and Ju-88 level-bombers wreaked havoc on Soviet lines of communications and helped to isolate the battlefield. At this point, German air-ground cooperation was at its apogee and the Luftwaffe's 'flying artillery' was a vital prerequisite for victory.

Axis satellite forces

Because of the inability of the German Ersatzheer to make good the losses of the winter fighting, Heeresgruppe Süd was forced to start using Romanian, Hungarian, Italian and Slovak troops to plug holes in the main front line. Hitherto, Axis allied troops had been used in secondary areas since the Germans doubted their capabilities and wanted to keep them away from decisive theatres of operation. Yet, by spring 1942, Heeresgruppe Süd was short almost 100,000 troops and Bock no longer had that luxury. The Hungarian 108th Light Infantry Division was committed in April to help AOK 6 contain Soviet forces in the Barvenkovo salient and remained holding a narrow sector in May. The Hungarian division had six infantry battalions and two artillery battalions, but its troops were only trained for rear-area security duties. Furthermore, the Hungarians were poorly equipped, having captured Belgian-made 47mm anti-tank guns and Czech-made 10cm howitzers.

The Romanians committed four infantry divisions (1, 2, 4, 20) under the 6th Corps headquarters, with a total of about 48,000 troops, to the Kharkov campaign. These Romanian units had not received a great deal of combat experience in the 1941 campaign and were particularly deficient in anti-tank weapons and artillery. Romanian infantry divisions were equipped with a mix of 3.7cm and 4.7cm anti-tank guns, neither of which was effective against Soviet T-34 tanks. The divisional artillery in Romanian divisions was based on 24–36 lightweight 7.5cm guns and 16–24 10cm howitzers, which gave them considerably less defensive fire than a German divisional artillery group.

The Italians contributed a cavalry group under Count Guglielmo Barbò di Caselmorano, consisting of two cavalry regiments, and a Bersaglieri Cyclist Battalion. Group Barbo was attached to the 1. Gebirgsjäger-Division. The Croatian Legion, designated as Infanterie-Regiment 369, was attached to the 100. leichte Infanterie-division. Formed in July 1941, the Croatian Legion was a reinforced infantry regiment with over 3,000 troops and its own artillery and anti-tank troops.

SOVIET

Tank corps

The Soviet Winter Counteroffensive had been conducted with only limited armour support, primarily relying on independent battalions and half-strength brigades. However, the Stavka realized that its pre-war deep battle doctrine could not be conducted with odds and ends, but required proper large mechanized formations to exploit breakthrough attacks. In early April 1942, the Red Army began forming a new series of tank corps, organized around three tank brigades and a motorized rifle brigade, with a nominal strength of 135–150 tanks. The main function of the tank corps was deep operations, while separate tank brigades were also maintained to support the infantry. In the Kharkov campaign, Timoshenko's armour was split between tank brigades embedded in each army for infantry support and two tank corps massed behind 6th Army as an exploitation force.

Soviet tank units in May 1942 had little conformity in terms of organization, training or equipment. The tank brigade was authorized 46 tanks and most of Timoshenko's tank units were at this strength, but they were equipped with a heterogeneous assortment of a dozen different tank models. While the best Soviet tanks – the heavy KV-1 and medium T-34 – were better than anything the Germans had, there were only 80 and 239 respectively of the 938 tanks assembled for the Kharkov offensive. Instead, the most numerous tanks were the T-60 light tanks, but their 20mm cannon

British-built Matilda II tanks arriving by rail prior to the offensive. Timoshenko was supplied with 117 Matilda II tanks and they were well suited to infantry support due to their thick frontal armour. (Author)

was insufficient to defeat German tanks. One-fifth of Timoshenko's tanks were comprised of British Lend-Lease tanks from convoys PQ-9/10/11, including 117 Matildas and 81 Valentines. The Matilda and Valentine were both well suited for infantry support work, so they were assigned to work in that role in independent brigades. However, the Soviets had few spares for British-made tanks, so their mechanical reliability was poor.

Soviet cavalry

The Red Army committed 12 cavalry divisions, grouped into four cavalry corps, to the Kharkov operation. According to the pre-war deep battle (*glubokiy boy*) doctrine codified in 1936, once Red Army rifle divisions and infantry support tank brigades broke through an enemy defensive line, large cavalry and mechanized formations should be pushed through the breach to conduct deep operations (*glubokaya operatsiya*) into the enemy rear areas to complete their destruction. In May 1942, the Red Army still only had modest large mechanized units and had to rely upon cavalry for the bulk of the exploitation mission. Based upon experience from earlier cavalry raids, each cavalry corps was given some artillery and a tank brigade to enable it to reduce enemy strongpoints, but Red cavalry lacked the firepower of a mechanized rifle formation. As a cavalryman himself, Timoshenko tended to favour his cavalry corps, but he did not understand that they no longer held the shock effect they had had during the Russian Civil War and their limitations on the modern battlefield were severe.

Red air support

At the beginning of the offensive on 12 May 1942, the VVS-South-Western Front had a three-to-one numerical superiority in fighters around Kharkov, although this was deceptive. The bulk of the Soviet fighters were Yak-1 and LaGG-3 types, with only a single regiment each of I-16 and MiG-3 fighters. While these fighters were roughly equal to the Bf-109F, Soviet pilots still lacked the training and experience to compete effectively against their Luftwaffe opponents. Superficially, the presence of four ground attack regiments with 67 Il-2 Sturmoviks and three bomber regiments with about 20–30 of the new Pe-2 bombers gave Timoshenko some very effective close air support at the outset. Nevertheless, nearly one-third of his air support from the VVS-South-Western Front consisted of obsolete U-2 biplane night bombers. Another glaring weakness was the pitiful number of reconnaissance aircraft assigned to the operation – only four – which made it difficult to detect the movement of German reserves. Furthermore, the available air support was too dispersed and uncoordinated, which prevented it from achieving operational-level results.

Artillery

When it came to deep battle, the Red Army believed that artillery was the god of war and they endeavoured to use massive amounts of it to batter their way through enemy defences. The four armies in the South-Western Front were provided 1,154 artillery pieces and 1,700 mortars for the offensive, including 224 152mm and 253 122mm howitzers. Timoshenko massed 40 per cent of his artillery to support 6th Army and 31 per cent to support 28th Army, leaving modest support for the 21st and 38th Armies. While these numbers were impressive by 1940 Russo-Finnish War standards, the

A Soviet 152mm M1937 (ML-20) howitzer prepares to fire. This corps artillery weapon was one of the best in the Soviet arsenal and had demonstrated its effectiveness against the Finnish Mannerheim Line. However, the ML 20 weighed nearly 8 tons and was poorly suited to supporting manoeuvre warfare. (Courtesy of the Central Museum of the Armed Forces, Moscow, via Stavka)

bulk of Timoshenko's artillery park comprised short-range mortars and 76.2mm guns. Heavy weapons such as the 152mm howitzer were needed to reduce German strongpoints, but they were still relatively few in number and supplied with less than half the ammunition needed for a sustained offensive.

ORDER OF BATTLE, 12 MAY 1942

GERMAN

HEERESGRUPPE SÜD (GENERALFELDMARSCHALL FEDOR VON BOCK)

Armeeoberkommando 6 (General der Panzertruppen Friedrich Paulus)

XXIX Armeekorps (General der Infanterie Hans Obstfelder)
    75. Infanterie-Division (IR 172)
    57. Infanterie-Division (-) (two regiments)
XVII Armeekorps (General der Infanterie Karl Strecker)
    79. Infanterie-Division (IR 212, 226)
        I, II, III/IR 429 (from 168. Infanterie-Division)
        III/IR 375 (from 221. Infanterie-Division)
        I/IR 529 (from 299. Infanterie-Division)
        294. Infanterie-Division (IR 513, 514)
        I, II, III/IR 211 (from 71. Infanterie-Division)
        II, III/IR 530 (from 299. Infanterie-Division)
        III/IR 164 and III/IR 183 (from 62. Infanterie-Division)
LI Armeekorps (General der Artillerie Walter von Seydlitz-Kurzbach)
    44. Infanterie-Division (IR 131, 132, 134)
    71. Infanterie-Division (IR 191, 211)

    297. Infanterie-Division (IR 522, 523, 524)
    3. Panzer-Division (reserve)
VIII Armeekorps (Generaloberst Walter Heitz)
    62. Infanterie-Division
        IR 208 (from 79. Infanterie-Division)
        IR 179 (from 57. Infanterie-Division)
        IR 515 (from 294. Infanterie-Division)
    454. Sicherungs-Division
    108th Light Infantry Division (Hungarian)
    Sturmgeschütz- Abteilung 244
AOK 6 RESERVES:
    113. Infanterie-Division (IR 260, 261, 268)
    23. Panzer-Division
Armee-Gruppe von Kleist (Generaloberst Ewald von Kleist)
Gruppe von Kortzfleisch
    XI Armeekorps (General der Infanterie Joachim von Kortzfleisch)
    298. Infanterie-Division
1./Panzerjäger-Abteilung 525 (6 Marder II)
VI Corps (Romanian) (General-Major Corneliu Dragalina)
    1st Infantry Division (Romanian)
    2nd Infantry Division (Romanian)

4th Infantry Division (Romanian)

20th Infantry Division (Romanian)

III Armeekorps (mot.) (Generaloberst Eberhard von Mackensen)

    14. Panzer-Division

    60. Infanterie-Division (mot.)

    1. Gebirgs-Division (incl. Italian Group Barbo, with two battalions)

    100. leichte Infanterie-division (Croatian IR 369 attached)

    Sturmgeschütz-Abteilung 245 (21 StuG III)

    Panzerjäger-Abteilung 670 (12 Marder II, 9 Panzerjäger I)

XXXXIV Armeekorps (General der Artillerie Maximilian de Angelis)

    16. Panzer-Division (attached 15 May)

    68. Infanterie-Division (Walloon Legion attached)

    97. leichte Infanterie-Division

    295. Infanterie-Division

    384. Infanterie-Division

LII Armeekorps (General der Infanterie Eugen Ott)

    101. leichte Infanterie-division

    257. Infanterie-Division

RESERVE:

    389. Infanterie-Division (-)

REINFORCEMENTS:

    305. Infanterie-Division, en route from Western Europe

    Kampfgruppe Gollwitzer from 88. Infanterie-Division, AOK 2

German operational tank strength, 12 May 1942

UNIT	PzKpfw II	PzKpfw III (short/long)	PzKpfw IV (short/long)	Total
3. Panzer-Division	9	27/13	10/11	70
23. Panzer-Division	34	62/50	26/6	178
14. Panzer-Division	14	42/24	22/0	102
16. Panzer-Division	14	42/25	16	97
TOTAL	47	325	91	447

LUFTWAFFE

Fliegerkorps IV (General Kurt Pflugbeil)

    III/JG 77 (40 x Bf 109F)

    KG 27 (30 x He-111H)

    II/KG 55 (30 x He-111H)

Reinforcements from the Crimea, 12–20 May:

III/JG 52 (26 x Bf-109F)

StG 77 (104 x Ju-87)

I, II, III/KG 51 (103 x Ju-88)

I/KG 76 (38 x Ju-88)

I/KG 77 (29 x Ju-88)

II/SchG 1 (43 x Hs 129 B-1)

II/JG 52 (40 x Bf 109F)

I/JG 3 (42 x Bf 109F)

I/JG 52 (36 x Bf 109F)

SOVIET

SOUTH-WESTERN FRONT (MARSHAL SEMEN K. TIMOSHENKO)

Chief of Staff: General-Lieutenant Ivan Bagramyan

21st Army (General-Major Vasiliy N. Gordov)

    76th Rifle Division

    227th Rifle Division

    293rd Rifle Division

    297th Rifle Division

    301st Rifle Division

    10th Tank Brigade (38 tanks)

    478th Separate Tank Battalion (22 tanks)

28th Army (General-Lieutenant Dmitri I. Ryabyshev)

    1st Echelon:

        13th Guards Rifle Division

        169th Rifle Division

        175th Rifle Division

        244th Rifle Division

        57th Tank Brigade (46 tanks)

        84th Tank Brigade (46 tanks)

        90th Tank Brigade (46 tanks)

    2nd Echelon:

        38th Rifle Division

        162nd Rifle Division

        6th Guards Tank Brigade (43 tanks)

        Mobile Group: 3rd Guards Cavalry Corps

        5th Guards Cavalry Division

        6th Guards Cavalry Division

        32nd Cavalry Division

        34th Motorized Rifle Brigade

38th Army (General-Major Kirill S. Moskalenko)

    81st Rifle Division

    124th Rifle Division

    199th Rifle Division

    226th Rifle Division

    300th Rifle Division

    304th Rifle Division

    13th Tank Brigade (44 tanks)

    36th Tank Brigade (47 tanks)

    133rd Tank Brigade (34 tanks)

6th Army (General-Lieutenant Avksentiy M. Gorodniansky)

    41st Rifle Division

    47th Mountain Rifle Division

    103rd Rifle Division

    248th Rifle Division

    253rd Rifle Division

    266th Rifle Division

    337th Rifle Division

    411th Rifle Division

    5th Guards Tank Brigade (38 tanks)

37th Tank Brigade (42 tanks)

38th Tank Brigade (44 tanks)

48th Tank Brigade (42 tanks)

21st Tank Corps (General-Major Grigoriy I. Kuzmin)

64, 198, 199th Tank Brigades (136 tanks)

4th Motorized Rifle Brigade

23rd Tank Corps (General-Major Efim G. Pushkin)

6, 130, 131 Tank Brigades (133 tanks)

23rd Motorized Rifle Brigade

Army Group Bobkin (General-Major Leonid V. Bobkin)

6th Cavalry Corps

26th Cavalry Division

28th Cavalry Division

49th Cavalry Division

7th Tank Brigade (40 tanks)

270th Rifle Division

393rd Rifle Division

912th Rifle Regiment (243 RD)

South-Western Front Reserves

2nd Cavalry Corps

38th Cavalry Division

62nd Cavalry Division

70th Cavalry Division

277th Rifle Division

343rd Rifle Division

71st, 92nd, 132nd Separate Tank Battalions (97 tanks)

58th Tank Brigade

SOUTHERN FRONT (GENERAL-LIEUTENANT RODION MALINOVSKY)

57th Army (General-Lieutenant Kuzma P. Podlas)

14th Guards Rifle Division

99th Rifle Division

150th Rifle Division

317th Rifle Division

351st Rifle Division

9th Army (General-Major Fedor M. Kharitonov)

51st Rifle Division

106th Rifle Division

333rd Rifle Division

335th Rifle Division

341st Rifle Division

349th Rifle Division

78th Rifle Brigade

12th Tank Brigade (ten tanks)

121st Tank Brigade (32 tanks)

Southern Front Reserves:

5th Cavalry Corps

30th Cavalry Division

34th Cavalry Division

60th Cavalry Division

12th Tank Brigade (ten tanks)

296th Rifle Division

3rd Tank Brigade

Stavka Reserve: 114th Tank Brigade

Soviet operational tank strength, 12 May 1942

UNIT	KV-1	T-34	BT	Matilda/Valentine	T-60	Other	Total
21st Army	6	4	8	0	0	42	60
28th Army	33	78	7	0	60	3	181
38th Army	0	22	29	28/20	17	9	125
Northern Group	39	104	44	28/20	77	54	366
6th Army	11	34	0	57/0	63	1	166
21st Tank Corps	20	38	0	10/20	48	0	136
23rd Tank Corps	0	58	0	0/30	45	0	133
AG Bobkin	7	5	10	0	17	1	40
Southern Group	38	135	10	67/50	173	2	475
9th Army	4	16	0	0	20	2	42

VVS-South-Western Front (General Fedor I. Falaleev)

Fighters (142)	148 IAP (MiG-3); 6, 146, 273, 282, 296, 429, 581, 929 IAP (Yak-1); 2, 23, 164, 168, 181, 248, 254, 512 IAP (LaGG-3); 43 IAP (I-16)
Night bombers (125)	596, 598, 709, 714 NBAP (U-2)
Day bombers (85)	52, 135 BAP (Su-2); 13GBAP, 99 BAP (Pe-2); 10 BAP (SB/Su-2/Pe-2)
Ground attack (67)	92, 211, 245, 431 ShAP (Il-2)

OPPOSING PLANS

SOVIET

After the culmination of the Soviet 1941/42 Winter Counteroffensive, the Soviet leadership was initially uncertain about whether to continue an offensive strategy into the warm weather months or to shift to the defensive. In the Stavka, Georgy Zhukov, Boris Shaposhnikov and Andrei Vasilevsky – expecting a renewed German offensive towards Moscow – urged caution. Zhukov realized that the Red Army desperately needed to rebuild its strength and did not want to waste the Stavka's limited strategic reserves on indecisive local attacks. Soviet industry was just beginning to replace the horrendous losses in tanks and artillery in 1941 and Zhukov wanted to conserve vital equipment and supplies until a decisive effort could be made, preferably with him in command. However, Stalin was more pugnacious after the partial successes of the Winter Counteroffensive and, by mid-March, he was inclined to believe that pre-emptive offensive action would enable the Red Army to retain the strategic initiative and thereby disrupt German plans for another attack on Moscow. Ignoring the General Staff's advice, Stalin not only decided to continue offensive operations in April–May 1942, but to conduct major attacks on multiple fronts in order to keep the Germans off-balance. Stalin was particularly in favour of resuming the offensive at Kharkov, where Moskalenko's seizure of the Staryi Saltov bridgehead convinced him that the German position there was vulnerable.

Soviet cavalry from the South-Western Front advancing, February 1942. Once Timoshenko achieved a breakthrough near Izyum in January, he committed three cavalry corps as an exploitation force. In a matter of weeks, the Soviet cavalry fanned out on diverging axes and created the Barvenkovo salient. However, the cavalry units lacked the firepower to overcome German strongpoints. (Ian Barter)

Situation on the Kharkov axis, 11 May 1942

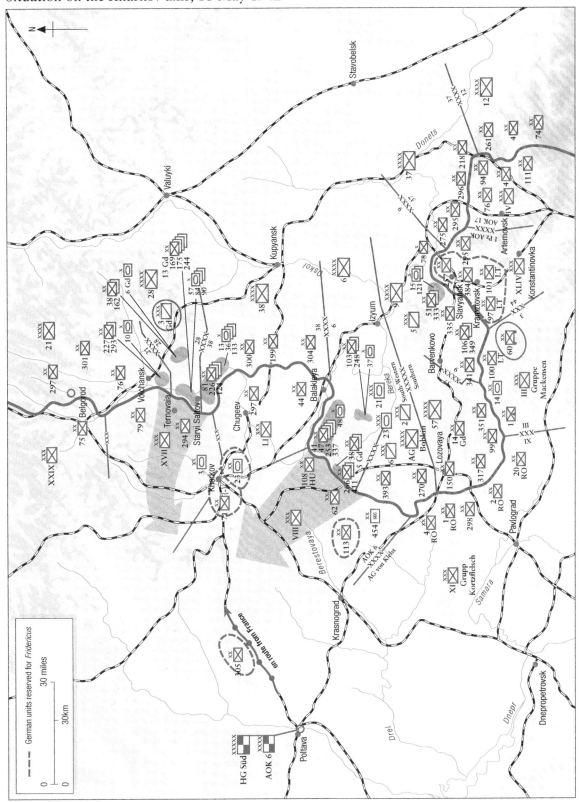

However, success tends to breed hubris in dictators and Stalin now saw opportunities for further success on the Volkhov, North-Western, Bryansk and Crimean Fronts as well. He promised reinforcements for each of these fronts, along with Timoshenko's South-Western Front, but there were simply not enough replacement troops and equipment to go around. Even with the arrival of significant Lend-Lease aid from Britain, tanks and artillery were still in short supply and Soviet industry was just ramping up after relocating to the Urals. Indeed, Stalin's decision to conduct multiple hastily planned offensives in spring 1942 ranks alongside his near-catastrophic decisions about Red Army deployments prior to *Barbarossa*. The senior officers in the Stavka were forced to grit their teeth in silence as Stalin dissipated their few reserves across too many fronts, pursuing too many objectives.

At South-Western Front headquarters, on 20 March Timoshenko had already ordered his chief of staff, General-Lieutenant Ivan Bagramyan, to begin planning for a major offensive against AOK 6 within the next six weeks. Once AOK 6 was eliminated, the South-Western Front would push on to the Dnepr. Although Soviet planning was undermined by politicized intelligence estimates, Timoshenko and Bagramyan were fully aware that the South-Western Front's depleted front-line forces were inadequate for an offensive of this scale without massive reinforcements. Bagramyan quickly wrote an outline plan as well as a long wish list of reinforcements, including 250,000 troops, 1,200 tanks and over 1,000 artillery pieces. A week later, Timoshenko and Bagramyan flew to Moscow to discuss the draft plan with Stalin and the Stavka. Although enthusiastic about another offensive at Kharkov, Stalin was stunned by the size of Timoshenko's request for reinforcements, which was equivalent to about five complete armies. Stalin demurred on approving Timoshenko's operational plan until it was rewritten and scaled down a bit, limiting the scope of the operation to the area immediately around Kharkov. On 10 April, Stalin and the Stavka approved the South-Western Front's revised plan, which stipulated that all preparations had to be completed by 6 May in order to pre-empt the Germans. A number of subordinate commanders had misgivings about the Red Army's ability to successfully organize and execute such a large-scale offensive with less than a month to prepare, but they held their tongues once it became obvious that Stalin had already made his decision. Indeed, in planning the Kharkov operation, senior Soviet officers in both the Stavka and at Timoshenko's South-Western Front headquarters acted more like robots than professional soldiers. Stalin said success was 'guaranteed', so they believed it.

LEFT
The Ukrainian mud had a major impact on degrading German mobility around Kharkov in autumn 1941 and spring 1942. The generally poor trafficability of Ukrainian rural roads severely impacted German logistics, making it difficult for AOK 6 to build up reserves of fuel and ammunition.
(Ian Barter)

RIGHT
Soviet infantry replacements move into the Barvenkovo salient in Spring 1942. The Soviet 6th Army was built up into a powerful assault force, but at the cost of stripping troops from the Southern Front's 9th and 57th Armies.
(From the fonds of the RGAKFD in Krasnogorsk via Stavka)

The basic plan for the South-Western Front offensive was premised on conducting a dual pincer attack, from the Barvenkovo salient and from the Staryi Saltov bridgehead. From the start, the plan had serious flaws. Rather than using Moskalenko's experienced 38th Army as the main effort in the north, Timoshenko brought in Ryabyshev's rebuilt 28th Army to spearhead his northern pincer. The 21st and 38th Armies would conduct supporting attacks to protect the 28th Army's flanks as it bludgeoned its way through the German defences towards Kharkov. While this meant that the daily operations of these three armies would have to be tightly coordinated, Timoshenko appointed no overall commander for the northern group. Furthermore, the northern group only received the 3rd Guards Cavalry Corps as an exploitation force, which was clearly insufficient for deep operations. In the south, the 6th Army was designated as the main effort, but Timoshenko created Army Group Bobkin from 6th Army resources on 27 April in order to provide a combined-arms flank guard for his main effort. However, this merely added more confusion to the Soviet command and control picture in the Barvenkovo salient, which was already split with 6th Army under South-Western Front but 9th and 57th Armies under Southern Front. From the beginning, Timoshenko's plan violated the basic principle of unity of command.

Timoshenko's staff planned for a deliberate operation to breach the German defences in depth as if they were attacking the Finnish Mannerheim Line two years prior, but failed to acknowledge that the Finns had lacked either mobile reserves or a powerful air force. Bagramyan and Timoshenko put their faith in massed artillery – not combined-arms operations – to settle the issue, as it had with the Finns. The Stavka sent Timoshenko 18 artillery regiments from its reserves and he stripped 14 regiments from Southern Front, provided him with over 1,000 medium calibre guns and howitzers. Once the German line was broken, strong mobile groups would be introduced to complete the victory by enveloping AOK 6. Timoshenko optimistically hoped to complete the encirclement of Kharkov and AOK 6 within 15 days of the beginning of the offensive. Two new tank corps, the 21st and 23rd Tank Corps, would push west to isolate Kharkov from the west and block any German relief effort. Throughout the planning stage, Timoshenko and Bagramyan paid little attention to the possibility that Armeegruppe von Kleist could shift any of its Panzers to counterattack the forces in the Barvenkovo salient and put little effort into contingency planning. Instead, Timoshenko directed Malinovsky's Southern Front to create a solid defensive line in front of Voroshilovgrad and Rostov and to plan for diversionary operations to tie down Kleist once South-Western Front began its offensive, but Malinovsky ignored Timoshenko's vague guidance. Vasilevsky was supposed to act as a coordinating agent on this operation for the Stavka, but he remained passively on the sidelines, failing to ensure both fronts could contribute to the success of the operation.

The South-Western Front began regrouping its forces for the operation on 10 April, but it took far longer to move up new units, replacements and supplies than expected. There were only two road bridges over the Donets supporting the armies in the Barvenkovo salient, which became logistical bottlenecks and prime targets for Luftwaffe interdiction sorties. About one-third of Soviet artillery was still en route and not in place at start of offensive, which reduced Timoshenko's main trump card. Given the limited time allotted, the logistic build-up for the offensive failed to meet planned requirements

A 122mm M30 howitzer being towed by a tractor. Timoshenko's plan was heavily shaped by his belief that massed artillery fire could smash the German defences – as he had done on the Finnish Mannerheim line two years before. (From the fonds of the RGAKFD in Krasnogorsk via Stavka)

and thus Timoshenko's forces were not ready for sustained combat by 6 May, as intended. Less than half the fuel and ammunition specified in the plan was assembled prior to the offensive. Timoshenko's main effort, the 6th Army, had three basic loads of 152mm ammunition, but less than two loads each of 122mm and 76.2mm. It was anticipated that the artillery would fire off at least one basic load on the first day, but it would have to be rationed afterwards. The 6th Army had less than three loads of fuel, even though Bagramyan anticipated needing seven to eight loads for the offensive. Even food rations were poorly distributed, with some units receiving just one or two days' worth of rations for a 15-day operation. It also took much longer to move up infantry and tank replacements, with the result that pre-battle training was minimal. The 28th Army headquarters arrived in sector in mid-April, which meant that its forces were the least organized when the offensive began. Although the Stavka had intended that Kharkov would be the Red Army's first carefully planned deliberate offensive of the war – unlike the ad hoc efforts of the previous six months – Stalin's impatience for action resulted in another hastily planned attack with inadequately trained and supplied forces. Zhukov and Vasilevsky looked on with foreboding, but said nothing.

On 28 April, the South-Western Front issued an updated offensive operations plan in Directive 00275. Recognizing that preparations were still incomplete, Timoshenko delayed the onset of the offensive to 12 May, but this made little difference. With the weather improving daily, Timoshenko

Soviet infantry training on moving through barbed-wire obstacles prior to the offensive. The new recruits were given a couple of weeks, at best, to learn basic infantry skills, but the rushed nature of the whole offensive precluded in-depth training. Later German post-battle assessments noted the lack of aggressiveness in many Soviet infantry units. (Author)

knew that he had to strike before the Germans launched their own offensive. Soviet intelligence estimates about the German forces around Kharkov greatly underestimated enemy forces and capabilities. Some German units, such as the 113. Infanterie-Division, were not even detected prior to the offensive. Timoshenko was particularly dismissive about Moskalenko's concerns that the two German Panzer divisions in reserve near Kharkov could quickly counterattack the forces advancing from the Staryi Saltov bridgehead. According to Timoshenko's wishful thinking, the Germans would not react for several days, allowing both assault groups adequate time to penetrate the German defensive lines and introduce their exploitation units.

GERMAN

While Stalin and the Stavka were formulating their plans for the Kharkov offensive, Hitler and the OKH were developing their own plans for the summer 1942 campaign. Soviet assumptions that the Germans would make another attempt on Moscow proved false. Instead, Hitler intended to conduct his main summer campaign in the south, with twin drives towards the Volga and the oilfields in the Caucasus. Once these objectives were achieved, Hitler believed that the Soviet war economy would collapse. Substantial reinforcements were being assembled for the grand offensive designated *Blau*, including larger contributions by Axis satellite troops. However, two vital operational prerequisites needed to be accomplished before Heeresgruppe Süd would be in a position to embark on a major campaign toward the Volga: the Soviet position in the Crimea had to be eliminated and Timoshenko's armies in the Barvenkovo salient destroyed. In Fuhrer Directive 41, dated 5 April 1942, Hitler provided guidance to Heeresgruppe Süd on both the Crimea and Kharkov preliminary operations and directed that, 'the enemy forces which have broken through on both sides of Izyum will be cut off along the course of the Donets River and destroyed.'

German troops in front-line positions prior to the Soviet offensive. Although stretched thin, the infantry of AOK 6 were well established in field works. (Ian Barter)

Even with reinforcements from the west, Bock recognized that it would take months to rebuild Heeresgruppe Süd's ground combat power and that both preliminary operations would have to rely heavily upon Luftwaffe air support. Given the limited number of squadrons available to Luftflotte 4, air units would have to be cycled between supporting Generaloberst Erich von Manstein's AOK 11 in the Crimea and Paulus' AOK 6 at Kharkov. Instead of being able to conduct simultaneous offensives as in 1941, the Germans were forced to conduct sequential operations in 1942. Furthermore, the bulk of reinforcements en route to the Eastern Front would not arrive until June 1942, meaning that the preliminary operations would have to rely upon the forces already available

Since late February, Bock had envisioned a classic pincer attack against the base of the Barvenkovo salient, using assault groups from AOK 6 and Armee-Gruppe von Kleist. However, due to the lack of sufficient air support or combat-ready Panzer units, it had been put off again and again. The OKH ordered the transfer of the 71. and 305. Infanterie-Divisionen from the west to Heeresgruppe Süd in March to provide AOK 6 with forces for the counterstroke, while Armee-Gruppe von Kleist had to rely upon its own resources. Retention of the vital Slavyansk and Balakleya hedgehogs at the base of the Barvenkovo salient provided the necessary springboards for the German counterstroke since, from these positions, the salient was just 75 km wide. Bock's staff in Dnepropetrovsk laid out the basis for the attack, which was designated *Fridericus*. Bock intended to execute *Fridericus* in mid-April, but continued Soviet attacks against the periphery of the salient made it difficult for either AOK 6 or Kleist to pull units out of the line to refit for an offensive. Originally, the AOK 6 pincer was supposed to be led by the 3. Panzer-Division, but since this unit was critical for containing the Soviet Staryi bridgehead, in mid-April the OKH sent Paulus the newly raised 23. Panzer-Division to join the three infantry divisions forming the assault group. Kleist's assault group would conduct the main attack from the south with five divisions, spearheaded by one or two Panzer divisions, depending upon availability. By 1941 standards, *Fridericus* was a fairly anaemic effort, involving a couple of half-strength Panzer divisions and a handful of tired infantry divisions. Unsure of success, Bock allowed the operation's date to slide backwards until more reinforcements arrived from the west. Paulus was nervous about the Soviet forces in the Staryi Saltov bridgehead and proposed using the 23. Panzer-Division to eliminate this threat in a spoiling attack designated *Westwind*, but Bock vetoed any diversions that could wreck his timetable.

Heeresgruppe Süd's strained logistic situation made planning for a large-scale offensive difficult. It had taken months for the Organization Todt to rebuild the railroad bridge at Dnepropetrovsk and the rail lines leading to Kharkov. Throughout the winter and into the spring thaw, Heeresgruppe Süd only received a thin trickle of fuel, ammunition and replacements since the OKH had given priority of logistical support to Heeresgruppe Mitte, which was in danger of collapse. The fuel situation was particularly critical. The basic load of fuel or Verbrauchssatz (abbreviated as one V.S) for a German division was the amount of petrol and diesel required to move all the division's vehicles 100km. German doctrine stated that a mechanized unit should have four V.S. on hand prior to an offensive. Yet, on 25 April 1942, the two main shock units of Gruppe Mackensen – the 14. Panzer-Division and 60. Infanterie-Division (mot.) – each had less than 0.2 V.S. of fuel. Without adequate fuel, no major

A German 15cm s.FH18 howitzer battery waits in concealed positions. Each German forward regiment had a battalion or more of artillery in direct support, ready to unleash a torrent of high explosive upon Soviet troops in the open. (Ian Barter)

attack could be launched. The situation was better with ammunition, with enough 10.5cm and 15cm artillery ammunition on hand in Armee-Group von Kleist to support up to a week of sustained offensive combat.

Fridericus was intended to be primarily an infantry attack backed by the Luftwaffe, with only modest levels of tank and artillery support. In order to gain more good-quality infantry for the assault groups, AOK 6 and Armee-Gruppe von Kleist gave the Romanian 6th Corps a larger sector on the Barvenkovo salient, which enabled the 113. Infanterie-Division to be pulled out of the line for refitting on 4 May. As of 5 May, the plan called for Armee-Group von Kleist to attack with elements of five infantry divisions (68, 257, 384, 97 leichte and 101 leichte) and 16. Panzer-Division (90 tanks), supported by about 200 medium howitzers. Paulus would attack with 23. Panzer-Division and three infantry divisions (71, 113 and 305). The plan directed Kleist's infantry divisions to carve out a path through the Soviet 9th Army from Slavyansk to Izyum, which the 16. Panzer-Division would push up through. The link-up with AOK 6's assault group would occur north of Izyum, hopefully trapping at least three Soviet armies in the salient. As part of the cycle of preliminary operations, Bock directed Manstein to commence operation *Trappenjagd* against the Soviet Kerch grouping on 8 May and AOK 11 would get the bulk of Luftwaffe support for about ten days. After *Trappenjagd* was completed, Luftflotte 4 would shift its aircraft back to the Kharkov area and X-tag for *Fridericus* was set for 18 May. Bock expected *Fridericus* to be completed by the end of May and then the Luftwaffe squadrons would return to the Crimea to support Manstein's attack on Sevastopol on 2 June. Thus, Heeresgruppe Süd was on a tight timeline and had to achieve success quickly in order for the goals of Fuhrer Directive 41 to be met.

Yet, unlike Timoshenko, Bock would not allow himself to be rushed into a premature offensive. He knew that the flat open terrain around Izyum favoured the German form of manoeuvre warfare and that the improving weather was, in itself, a harbinger of success. Heeresgruppe Süd would only attack when it had the best prospects for victory. Nor did Hitler put the kind of stress on Bock that Stalin put on Timoshenko; as long as Heeresgruppe Süd was ready to begin its drive to the Volga by late June, he would not interfere with the conduct of the preliminary operations. However, Bock was guilty of believing that Timoshenko would not launch his own offensive until he was equally ready and the Soviet willingness to conduct an attack with forces that were not fully assembled surprised him.

THE SOVIET OFFENSIVE, 12–16 MAY 1942

'This is no blemish in the line, rather our very existence is at stake'

Bock to Halder

Apparently unconcerned about the possibility of a major Soviet offensive, Paulus decided that the evening of 11/12 May would be an appropriate time for a dinner party at his headquarters in Kharkov with his subordinate corps commanders. Yet, unknown to him, just 30km away Timosheno's forces were preparing to launch one of the largest Soviet set-piece offensives of the war to date. Some German front-line commanders were aware that 'something was up' because there had been indications of increased Soviet activity for the past several days. Deserters had been crossing the lines warning of an imminent offensive. The 21st Army had been particularly active, with its 76th Rifle Division infiltrating an assault group across the Donets near Bezliudovka in order to gain a foothold to support the upcoming main attack. The German 79. Infanterie-Division conducted local counterattacks to contain the crossing and Paulus was satisfied that he had the situation in hand. On 11 May, the VVS-South-Western Front began to conduct aggressive fighter-bomber raids on Fliegerkorps IV airfields around Kharkov, but these attacks failed to cause any real damage.

THE NORTHERN GROUP, 12–20 MAY 1942

General der Infanterie Karl Strecker's XVII Armeekorps had two infantry divisions, the 79. and 294. Infanterie-Divisionen deployed on a 48km-wide sector between Grafovka and Bolshaya Babka to oppose the main offensive might of the Soviet 21st, 28th and 38th Armies. Strecker's troops were thinly spread and they only had a lightly held security zone in front of their *Hauptkampflinie* (HKL), which was anchored on battalion-size *Stutzpünkte* (strongpoints) in villages and towns. Barbed-wire obstacles were in place to slow infantry attacks, along with some anti-tank mines, but the defence rested on the concerted employment of automatic weapons and artillery to shred Soviet attacks. Since the beginning of the effort to contain the Soviet Staryi Saltov bridgehead in March, these two divisions had been supplemented with battalions from five other divisions and were now a hodgepodge that undermined unit cohesion. In the centre, the 294. Infanterie Division had ten infantry battalions, which were deployed along the HKL in four mixed-arms groups. Since the 294. Infanterie-Division had very limited anti-tank defences – just 40 3.7cm and six 5cm Pak – the Germans were forced to deploy artillery batteries well forward to supplement the *Panzerjäger*. The 79. Infanterie had 11 infantry battalions deployed to cover both the northern

end of the Staryi Saltov bridgehead as well as the Donets River front. Although Strecker had virtually no reserves, aside from a couple of pioneer companies and two 8.8cm Flak guns, Oberst Hermann Barnbeck's IR 211 from the 71. Infanterie-Division had just been relieved by the 294. Infanterie-Division's IR 513 and was located west of Peremoga. About 25km behind Strecker's HKL, AOK 6 had the 3. and 23. Panzer-Divisionen in reserve, but these units had been set aside for the upcoming *Fridericus* and could not be committed to local actions without the approval of the OKH. The LI AK held Bolshaya Babka with III/IR 522 from the 297. Infanterie-Division.

It began getting light just after 0430hrs, with sunrise occurring near 0500hrs. It would be a sunny day with clear skies and temperatures reaching 71° F (22° C). As soon as they could observe the German lines, the Soviet forward observers began directing ranging fire, which alerted AOK 6's front-line troops. At 0630hrs, over 800 artillery pieces, heavy mortars and multiple rocket launchers from the 21st, 28th and 38th Armies began pounding the front-line units of AOK 6's XVII and LI AK. The 60-minute-long artillery preparation extended across a 50km-wide front and to a depth of 5km. Although the Soviets fired off tens of thousands of rounds in this preparation, its effects varied from sector to sector. Relatively few German troops were killed by the bombardment, but the *landsers* – who had rarely experienced concentrated Soviet barrages in the past – were stunned. Just as the bombardment tapered off, Soviet Il-2 Sturmoviks and Pe-2 bombers swooped in to attack German artillery emplacements and *Stutzpünkte* just behind the front line. Meanwhile, Soviet fighters established air superiority over the northern front, with no opposition from the Luftwaffe. The VVS-South-Western Front conducted 660 sorties on the first day of the offensive, mostly over the northern sector. The only real opposition came from German Flak, which succeeded in shooting down seven Soviet aircraft.

Although the ground assault was not supposed to begin until 0730hrs, both the 28th and 38th Armies allowed units to begin advancing under cover of the artillery. The centrepiece of these attacks were six division-size shock groups, each with three rifle regiments, a tank brigade and the support of an artillery

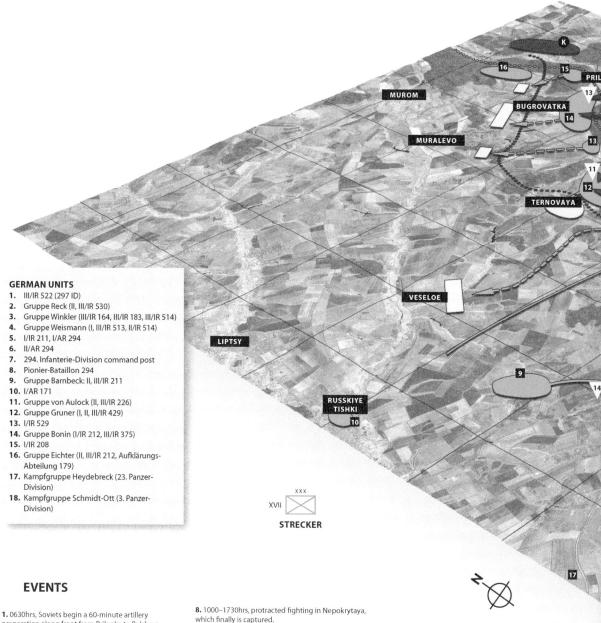

GERMAN UNITS

1. III/IR 522 (297 ID)
2. Gruppe Reck (II, III/IR 530)
3. Gruppe Winkler (III/IR 164, III/IR 183, III/IR 514)
4. Gruppe Weismann (I, III/IR 513, II/IR 514)
5. I/IR 211, I/AR 294
6. II/AR 294
7. 294. Infanterie-Division command post
8. Pionier-Bataillon 294
9. Gruppe Barnbeck: II, III/IR 211
10. I/AR 171
11. Gruppe von Aulock (II, III/IR 226)
12. Gruppe Gruner (I, II, III/IR 429)
13. I/IR 529
14. Gruppe Bonin (I/IR 212, III/IR 375)
15. I/IR 208
16. Gruppe Eichter (II, III/IR 212, Aufklärungs-Abteilung 179)
17. Kampfgruppe Heydebreck (23. Panzer-Division)
18. Kampfgruppe Schmidt-Ott (3. Panzer-Division)

EVENTS

1. 0630hrs, Soviets begin a 60-minute artillery preparation along front from Prilepka to Bolshaya Babka.

2. 0640–0800hrs, Gorbatov's 226th Rifle Division routs Gruppe Winkler.

3. Rodimstev's 13th Guards Rifle Division routs Gruppe Weissmann.

4. 781st Rifle Regiment from 124th Rifle Division envelops Gruppe Reck.

5. Remainder of 124th Rifle Division crosses river Babka south of Peschanoye.

6. 81st Rifle Division initially repulsed at Bolshaya Babka but finally captures town.

7. 294. Infanterie-Division commits its pioneer battalion to reinforce Gruppe Weissmann.

8. 1000–1730hrs, protracted fighting in Nepokrytaya, which finally is captured.

9. 1220hrs, Gruppe Reck forced to withdraw.

10. Gruppe von Aulock forced to withdraw towards Veseloe after Bayrak overrun.

11. 175th Rifle Division encircles German *Stützpunkt* at Varvarovka.

12. Oberst Grüner (IR 429) counterattacks and routs 556th Rifle Regiment.

13. 227th and 293rd Rifle Divisions force back Gruppe Bonin and advance toward Murom.

14. Gruppe Barnbeck (IR 211) ordered to establish blocking positions west of Nepokrytaya.

15. Evening, Kampfgruppe Schmidt-Ott from 3. Panzer-Division arrives in assembly area near Privol'e.

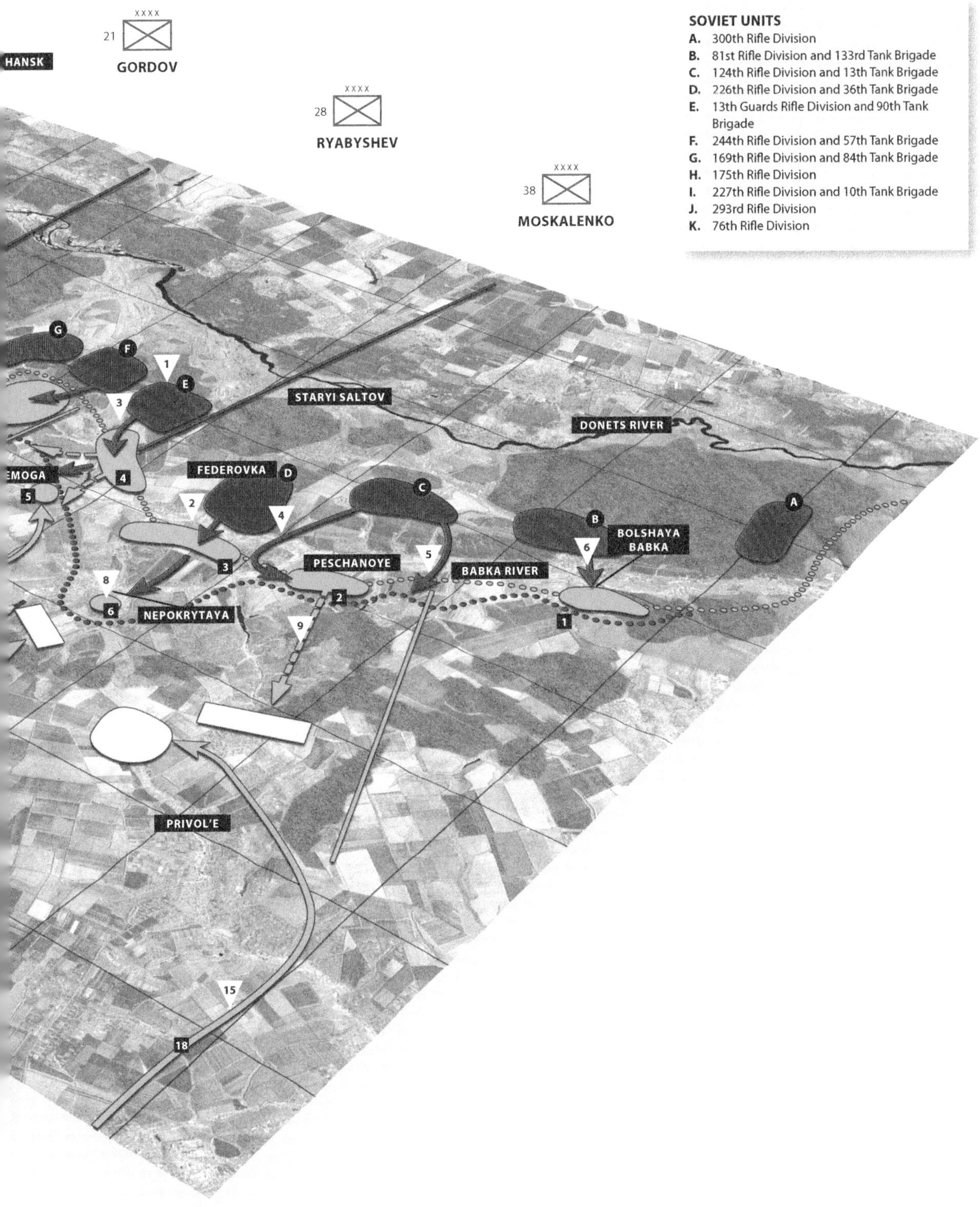
XXXX
21
GORDOV
XXXX
28
RYABYSHEV
XXXX
38
MOSKALENKO
SOVIET UNITS
A. 300th Rifle Division
B. 81st Rifle Division and 133rd Tank Brigade
C. 124th Rifle Division and 13th Tank Brigade
D. 226th Rifle Division and 36th Tank Brigade
E. 13th Guards Rifle Division and 90th Tank Brigade
F. 244th Rifle Division and 57th Tank Brigade
G. 169th Rifle Division and 84th Tank Brigade
H. 175th Rifle Division
I. 227th Rifle Division and 10th Tank Brigade
J. 293rd Rifle Division
K. 76th Rifle Division
STARYI SALTOV
DONETS RIVER
FEDEROVKA
PESCHANOYE
BABKA RIVER
BOLSHAYA BABKA
NEPOKRYTAYA
PRIVOL'E

ATTACK OF THE SOVIET NORTHERN GROUP, 12 MAY 1942

Three Soviet armies attack the German XVII AK but fail to achieve a major breakthrough on the first day of the offensive.

regiment, or a total of 3,500–4,000 infantry and 40–45 tanks. General-Major Aleksandr Rodimstev's 13th Guards Rifle Division was the strongest shock group and also had a pioneer battalion for clearing mines and a multiple rocket launcher battalion. Rodimstev's division attacked Gruppe Weissmann, which was holding *Stützpunkte* in the villages of Dragunovka and Kup'evakha. This group, with two battalions of IR 513, was badly stunned by the bombardment and, by the time that they recovered their senses, Rodimstev's pioneers had cleared lanes through their barbed wire and minefields. The Soviet guardsmen executed a classic set-piece attack, with one rifle regiment and tank battalion assaulting each *Stützpunkt*. The 90th Tank Brigade had a company each of KV-1 and T-34 tanks, which Gruppe Weissman's two 5cm Pak guns could not stop. Indeed, the Achilles heel of the German defence that morning was the feebleness of the *Panzerjäger* in the face of Soviet heavy tanks. Once the German infantrymen realized that they were being overrun, they were seized with the kind of 'tank panic' that had afflicted the French in 1940 and they began to abandon their positions in Dragunovka and Kup'evakha without permission. Two German artillery batteries fired their remaining ammunition, knocking out a couple of tanks, but then destroyed their own guns and retreated as well. In just a few hours of fighting, Gruppe Weissmann had dissolved into a pack of fleeing refugees and Rodimtsev whipped his men into pursuit towards Peremoga. On his left flank, General-Major Aleksandr Gorbatov's 226th Rifle Division achieved almost unbelievable success due to a carefully planned artillery bombardment that suppressed Gruppe Winkler's defensive positions overwatching the ford sites above the Babka River near Fedorovka. Gorbatov was a former Tsarist NCO with a wealth of combat experience and a meticulous planner. Incredibly, Gorbatov managed to get a rifle battalion and 14 tanks from the 36th Tank Brigade across the Babka River by 0640hrs without loss. Racing towards the German positions on Hill 199 guarding the approaches to Nepokrytaya, Gorbatov's infantry and tanks overran Gruppe Winkler's outposts before they could put up effective resistance. Gorbatov shoved more troops and tanks across the Babka, enabling him to seize the high ground by 0800hrs. Gruppe Winkler's *Panzerjäger*, with only a single 5cm Pak, were quickly outfought by the 30 Matilda and Valentine tanks of the 36th Tank Brigade, which incited another 'tank panic'. Gruppe Winkler's infantry began to fall back towards Kharkov, exposing the left flank of Gruppe Reck in Peschanoe.

Amazingly, two of the 294. Infanterie Division's *Kampfgruppen* had been routed due to the sudden appearance of large numbers of tanks that their *Panzerjäger* could not stop. Strecker quickly committed his limited reserves, two engineer companies, to seal the gaps created by the defeat of Gruppe Weissmann and Winkler. In Nepokrytaya, Oberst Herbert Winkler still had his regimental command post in the town, but very little infantry. Gorbatov pushed two tank companies into the east edge of the town, but ran into unexpected difficulty when two German l.FH 18 howitzer batteries engaged his British-made tanks with direct fire. Six tanks were immobilized and Gorbatov was forced to break off his attack until his infantry could catch up. Meanwhile, a handful of German officers – including two supply officers – established a collection point outside Nepokrytaya and began to coral some of Winkler's fleeing infantrymen and send them back into the town. The result was a protracted street fight in Nepokrytaya that cost both sides dearly, with 12 of the 36th Tank Brigade's tanks knocked out but two German artillery batteries destroyed as well. Gorbatov's infantry finally took possession of Nepokrytaya around 1730hrs.

Moskalenko's two other shock groups crossed the Babka River further south, pushing back the 294. Infanterie-Division's right flank. The 124th Rifle Division and 13th Tank Brigade managed to envelop Gruppe Reck in Stützpunkt Peschanoe, forcing it to withdraw westwards by 1220hrs. However, Gruppe Reck's withdrawal was more orderly and it inflicted significant casualties, since IR 530 had been one of the first units to receive the new MG42 machine gun. At Bolshaya Baka, the 81st Rifle Division initially committed only a single regiment and some tanks to attacking III/IR 522's *Stützpunkt* and suffered heavy losses, including 11 tanks. Moskalenko had hoped to keep the other two rifle regiments as a reserve for his main effort, but was forced to commit both to capture Bolshaya Babka. Due to this decision, the 38th Army was left with no appreciable reserves.

GERMAN ARTILLERIE-REGIMENT 294 HOWITZERS ENGAGE SOVIET 36TH TANK BRIGADE MATILDA TANKS IN STREETS OF NEPOKRYTAYA, 1100HRS, 12 MAY 1942 (PP. 40–41)

Owing to the poor performance of the standard German 3.7cm and 5cm Pak guns against Soviet heavy tanks, Paulus' AOK 6 was often forced to use massed artillery to stop Soviet tank attacks. On the morning of 12 May 1942, the Saxon 294. Infanterie-Division faced the brunt of the Soviet 28th and 38th Army's offensive, which included over 260 tanks. Gruppe Winkler, comprising three infantry battalions and a *Panzerjäger* company, was defending Hill 199 just east of the important road junction in the town of Nepokrytaya when it was attacked by the Soviet 226th Rifle Division and the 36th Tank Brigade. When the group's only 5cm Pak gun was knocked out, the infantry were helpless against the Matilda and Valentine tanks of the 36th Tank Brigade. German infantry panicked and bolted for the rear, leaving the town virtually undefended.

Two Soviet tank companies raced into the town hard on the heels of the retreating German infantry but came under direct fire from 10.5cm l.FH18 howitzers **(1)** from the 4. and 5. Batterien of Artillerie-Regiment 294. Caught in the narrow streets of the town,

six of the British-built tanks were immobilized and set afire by the artillerymen **(2)**. Firing PzGr. armour-piercing rounds, the l.FH18 could defeat the Matilda II's thick frontal at ranges of 500–600m, but this required a certain amount of luck and precision. The Matilda II was equipped with a 2-pounder (40mm) gun that lacked a high-explosive round, which made it difficult for them to neutralize an enemy artillery battery. Without infantry support, the 36th Tank Brigade was forced to break off the attack until the 226th Rifle Division caught up. However, the Soviet tanks soon returned and fought the German batteries for several more hours, with both sides suffering losses. Eventually, the German artillerymen expended all their ammunition and were forced to blow up their remaining howitzers. Since German divisional howitzers were horse drawn, they had little ability to conducting a withdrawal under fire. The Soviets captured the town of Nepokrytaya before dusk – one of their big successes of the first day of the offensive. Later, Bock was chagrined that AOK 6 lost 16 batteries worth of artillery in the first three days of the Soviet offensive.

On the northern side of the Staryi Saltov bridgehead, Ryabyshev attacked with his other three first-echelon divisions. The 244th Rifle Division and 57th Tank Brigade contributed to the defeat of Gruppe Weissmann, and then advanced towards Peremoga. The 169th Rifle Division achieved considerable success in its sector and directed one rifle regiment to envelop IR 211 in Bayrak, while the other lead regiment boldly advanced westwards to seize important high ground to the northwest. After a tough fight, the Soviet tanks and infantry fought their way into Bayrak and II/IR 514 was compelled to withdraw. However, Gruppe Grüner at Ternovaya used a battalion from IR 429 to counterattack the over-extended Soviet 556th Rifle Regiment and routed it. Grüner's counterattack helped Gruppe von Aulock to withdraw its two battalions, but could not prevent the 175th Rifle Division from encircling the *Stützpunkt* in Varvarovka by the end of the day. The commander of the 294. Infanterie-Division tried to order Gruppe Barnbeck (IR 211) to reinforce the crumbling situation around Peremoga, but Barnbeck ignored his subordination to Gruppe Weissmann, which led to confusion and delay. Eventually, the closest battalion to Peremoga, I/IR 211, arrived back in the town just before Rodimstev's troops. With the help of I/AR 294, this battalion and the remnants of IR 513 managed to hold the town for the rest of the day.

General-Major Vasiliy N. Gordov's 21st Army conducted supporting attacks across the northern Donets with the 227th and 293rd Rifle Divisions, supported by the 10th Tank Brigade against the 79. Infanterie-Division's IR 226. After a successful river crossing, these units captured *Stützpunkte* in Bugrovatka and Staritsa from Gruppe Bonin. Although the 76th Rifle Division was able to expand its earlier bridgehead across the Donets, Gordov's two bridgeheads were not able to link up on the first day of the offensive.

After a very successful morning, the three Soviet armies spent most of the afternoon and early evening consolidating their gains. It had been a good day for the Red Army, with moderate losses. The commitment of 300 tanks had shattered the fragile German defence and enabled the Soviet shock groups to seize almost all the German front-line positions. The XVII AK had suffered significant, but not catastrophic damage. While the 294. Infanterie-Division's defence had proved rather shabby, it had avoided annihilation by abandoning ground.

In Kharkov, Paulus watched the Soviet offensive and reports of his infantry fleeing with dismay. He immediately turned to Bock and the Luftwaffe for help. Bock recognized that AOK 6 was dealing with a major enemy effort and not some local attack, so he gained permission from the

LEFT
Timoshenko also had 81 British-built Valentine infantry support tanks. These belong to the 36th Tank Brigade in 38th Army, which defeated Gruppe Winkler and seized Nepokrytaya on the first day of the offensive. (Courtesy of the Central Museum of the Armed Forces, Moscow, via Stavka)

RIGHT
Soviet *desant* infantry de-bark from a Matilda tank prior to assaulting a German position. Note the soldier with an SVT-40 rifle, indicating that this could be a guards unit. This type of tank-infantry-artillery coordination was rare for the Red Army in early 1942. (RIA Novosti, 491038)

Operations in the northern sector, 13–20 May 1942

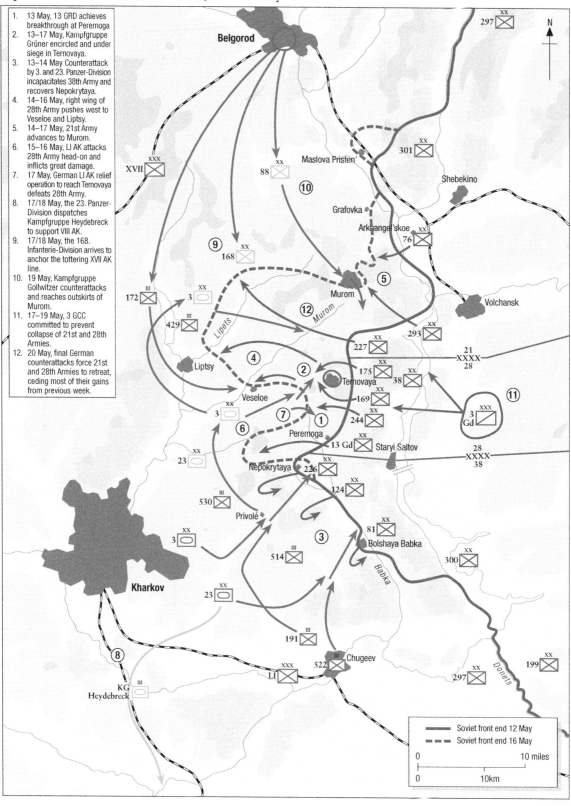

1. 13 May, 13 GRD achieves breakthrough at Peremoga
2. 13–17 May, Kampfgruppe Grüner encircled and under siege in Ternovaya.
3. 13–14 May Counterattack by 3. and 23. Panzer-Division incapacitates 38th Army and recovers Nepokrytaya.
4. 14–16 May, right wing of 28th Army pushes west to Veseloe and Liptsy.
5. 14–17 May, 21st Army advances to Murom.
6. 15–16 May, LI AK attacks 28th Army head-on and inflicts great damage.
7. 17 May, German LI AK relief operation to reach Ternovaya defeats 28th Army.
8. 17/18 May, the 23. Panzer-Division dispatches Kampfgruppe Heydebreck to support VIII AK.
9. 17/18 May, the 168. Infanterie-Division arrives to anchor the tottering XVII AK line.
10. 19 May, Kampfgruppe Gollwitzer counterattacks and reaches outskirts of Murom.
11. 17–19 May, 3 GCC committed to prevent collapse of 21st and 28th Armies.
12. 20 May, final German counterattacks force 21st and 28th Armies to retreat, ceding most of their gains from previous week.

Belgorod

Maslova Pristen'

Shebekino

Grafovka

Arkhangel'skoe

Murom

Volchansk

Liptsy

Veseloe

Ternovaya

Peremoga

Staryi Saltov

Nepokrytaya

Privolé

Bolshaya Babka

Kharkov

Chugeev

Heydebreck

Soviet front end 12 May
Soviet front end 16 May

0   10 miles
0   10km

OKH to release the 23. Panzer-Division to counterattack Soviet forces that had crossed the Babka River. By 1000hrs, the 23. Panzer-Division was moving towards Bolshaya Babka with Kampfgruppe Heydebreck (two Panzer battalions, one *Panzergrenadier* battalion and one artillery battalion) and Kampfgruppe Kieler (SR 126 with one Panzer company and one artillery battery), both of which would be in a position to counterattack by the next morning. Paulus ordered LI AK to send the 3. Panzer-Division and three infantry regiments (IR 131, IR 191, IR 522) to reinforce XVII AK's right flank, while he ordered XXIX AK to transfer several units to reinforce the 79. Infanterie-Division. Due to the rapid success of Operation *Trappenjagd* in the Crimea, the Luftwaffe was also able to begin transferring units back to the Kharkov region to put a stop to the relentless Soviet air attacks. Yet, while the German response was prompt, Strecker's XVII AK still had to try and rebuild some kind of new front line until help arrived. The 294. Infanterie-Division was in chaos, with only Oberst Barnbeck's IR 211 still in fighting shape. Strecker directed him to establish blocking positions 3–4km west of Nepokrytaya and at Peremoga. The 79. Infanterie-Division was in slightly better shape. Strecker ordered Oberst Grüner's IR 429 to hold Stützpunkt Ternovaya and Gruppe Bonin to hold Murom.

13 May

The next morning brought another warm and sunny day. All three Soviet armies had regrouped during the night and resumed attacking shortly after dawn. Rodimstev's 13th GRD had reached the edge of Peremoga the previous evening and Ryabyshev provided him with a fresh rifle regiment from the second echelon 38th Rifle Division to assault the town. The remnants of Gruppe Weissmann combined with I/IR 211 and tried to organize a defence of Peremoga, but they were badly outgunned. Rodimtsev launched a concentric attack on the town with two rifle regiments and the 90th Tank Brigade. The result was another disaster for the Germans, with much of the infantry fleeing and the six 15cm howitzers of 12./AR 294 overrun. Gruppe Weissman was eliminated from the German order of battle. Flushed with success, Rodimtsev pushed his division west another 5km to the outskirts of Petrovkoe, where they were halted by German artillery and engineers. While Rodimtsev advanced westwards, the 244th Rifle Division and 57th Tank Brigade on his right flank advanced pushed north-west towards Veseloe. A Soviet air strike bombed the command post of the German 294. Infanterie-Division, further paralyzing the battered Saxon division.

While Rodimtsev was enjoying great success, the rest of Ryabyshev's 28th Army focused on crushing German resistance at Ternovaya. Soviet tanks had begun to envelop the town from the south and the 200-man outpost at Varvarovka was overrun early in the morning. Oberst Grüner occupied a much stronger position in Ternovaya than the other German *Stutzpünkte*; in addition to his three infantry battalions, he had a Panzer company with eight PzKpfw III tanks, two 5cm Pak and an artillery battery, a total of about 2,000 troops. Ryabyshev directed the 169th and 175th Rifle Divisions to complete the encirclement of Ternovaya and then launch a full-scale attack on the town. Grüner conducted a skilful delaying action outside the town that delayed encirclement for much of the day. The VVS conducted a major 30-plane air raid on the town, but since Ryabyshev viewed Ternovaya as a mop-up action, he committed only minimal armour support. The result was that Grüner held and succeeded in tying up a major larger force for the bulk of a day. Frustrated, Ryabyshev ordered the second-echelon 38th Rifle Division, which had only two of its regiments, to continue the siege of Ternovaya, while the 169th and 175th Rifle Divisions continued their advance westwards. Ryabyshev's failure to recognize that the importance of committing adequate forces to achieve rapid and decisive results at Ternovaya would have fateful consequences for the entire Soviet northern attack group.

Further north, Gordov's 21st Army had a good day, with the 76th and 293rd Rifle Divisions finally linking up to join their bridgeheads. Yet, when these divisions began pushing westwards, they encountered stiff resistance from the 79. Infanterie-Division's *Stutzpünkte* at Murom and Grafovka. Lacking tank support, they had to await their artillery moving up before attacking. South of Murom, Gordov's 227th Rifle Division and 10th Tank Brigade found a weak spot in 79. Infanterie-Division's defence and advanced boldly 6km to capture Muralevo and Vysokii.

In the 38th Army sector, Moskalenko was concerned by intelligence reports indicating that German Panzer units were moving in his direction and he recommended caution. Timoshenko ordered him to continue his army's offensive but, in order to deal with any German counterattack, Moskalenko was directed to hold back the 13th, 36th and 133rd Tank Brigades and form them into the ad hoc 22nd Tank Corps. The result of this idiotic decision was that Moskalenko's three shock groups continued forwards without adequate tank support. Yet, even without tanks, Gruppe Barnbeck's three infantry battalions could do little to stop Moskalenko's push towards Michailovka and Chervona-Roganka. By 1200hrs, Gorbatov's 226th Rifle Division was within 18km of Kharkov. It was at this point, with the 294. Infanterie-Division's defence completely broken and the way open to Kharkov, that the Germans launched their first major counterattack. Seydlitz's LI AK directed the operation. The Germans had prepared their riposte carefully, waiting for both the Luftwaffe and IR 131 and IR 191 to arrive before moving. The III/JG 52 had just returned from the Crimea and around 1130hrs it conducted a fighter sweep east of Kharkov that shot down at least eight Soviet fighters for the loss of one Bf-109, which caused the VVS to retreat from the skies over 38th Army. Around 1230hrs, Kampfgruppe Schmitt-Ott from 3. Panzer-Division (III/Panzer-Regiment 6 and I/Schützen Regiment 3) and IR 191 struck the 124th Rifle Division at Chervona-Roganka, while 23. Panzer-Division and IR 131 hit the 81st Rifle Division west of Bolshaya Babka. Both Soviet infantry divisions were caught in the open by Panzers and shattered. Soviet artillery tried to stop the Panzers with direct fire and

T-34 tanks from the 5th Guards Tank Brigade support an attack on a village near Velikaya Bereka, which was held by IR 208. Against Timoshenko's expectations, the German 62. Infanterie-Division managed to prevent 6th Army from achieving a decisive breakthrough in its sector before Bock could commit his reserves. (Author)

succeeded in knocking out two or three from 3. Panzer-Division before being overrun. The battered Soviet infantry fell back towards Michailovka and Nepokrytaya, forcing Gorbatov's 226th Rifle Division to pull back as well. Moskalenko committed part of 22nd Tank Corps to support the retreat, which cost it ten tanks. The day ended with 38th Army knocked back on its heels and having suffered about 5,000 casualties. Of the 262 German Panzers involved in the counterattack, only three were destroyed and 19 temporarily out of action – an 8 per cent loss rate.

The setback suffered by 38th Army was the first indication that Timoshenko's plan had miscalculated the German response. When faced with the unexpected, good commanders employ what Napoleon and Clausewitz called *coup d'œil* to grasp the essence of the situation and take rapid action to regain the initiative. Poor commanders simply shift units around, sometimes in random fashion. Unfortunately for the Red Army, Timoshenko lacked *coup d'œil* and he decided to transfer most of Ryabyshev's second echelon, the 162nd Rifle Division and 6th Guards Tank Brigade, to reinforce Moskalenko's 38th Army. Yet Ryabyshev's only remaining second-echelon force, the 38th Rifle Division, was already committed to reducing the Ternovaya *Stützpunkt*. Incredibly, Timoshenko had decided to 'reinforce failure' in the 38th Army sector, while depriving his main effort in the 28th Army of the resources to sustain its advance towards Kharkov. Timoshenko lamely promised Ryabyshev a rifle division from the South-Western Front reserves, but this would not arrive for four days. The only significant uncommitted force left to the Soviet northern assault group was the 3rd Guards Cavalry Corps, which sat uselessly in the rear. After achieving significant success, the Red Army felt the initiative slipping from its grasp by the end of the second day of the offensive.

14 May

14 May brought another warm, sunny day and the Luftwaffe made the most of it. In addition to more fighters, StG 77 returned from the Crimea with about 100 Ju-87 Stukas and these were directed to support the LI AK counterattack against 38th Army. Overhead, the VVS retreated, stung by the loss of another eight fighters and unable to compete with Luftwaffe Bf-109 *Experten*. With local air superiority in hand, 3. and 23. Panzer-Divisionen, supported by two infantry regiments, continued their attack. The 23. Panzer-Division was able to encircle a rifle regiment from the 81st Rifle Division and reach the Babka River without much difficulty, but the 3. Panzer-Division became involved in a protracted battle with the 124th and 226th Rifle Divisions around Nepokrytaya. It was not until 1730hrs that Kampfgruppe Schmidt-Ott recaptured the town and the last Soviet infantry retreated behind the Babka. During the day, Moskalenko committed his remaining armour in driblets, accomplishing little but the loss of ten more tanks. The counterattack by LI AK had been a complete success that removed the 38th Army from the Soviet offensive line-up.

Despite this German victory, the Soviet northern group was still in a position to inflict a great deal of damage. The centre of XVII AK's sector was in a state of flux, with a 12km-wide sector west of Peremoga held by only four battalion-size remnants from the 294. Infanterie-Division. Ryabyshev advanced against this thin grey line with four rifle divisions (169, 175, 244 and 13th Guards) and two tank brigades (57, 84), but was forced to leave the 90th Tank Brigade to defend Peremoga against LI AK's Panzers coming from the south. The remnants of Gruppe Winkler delayed as best they could but abandoned Veseloe and fell back towards the Murom River. Ryabyshev's forces advanced 4–6km but failed to crush Winkler's rearguard. At this point in the battle, Ryabyshev faced only remnants between his spearheads and Kharkov, but lacked the reserves or exploitation force to complete the victory. Timoshenko's decision to hold back armour and divert second-echelon forces to deal with the German counterattack now robbed the entire northern offensive of its one chance for decisive success.

Ryabyshev hoped to get the 38th Rifle Division back into the fight, but its attack on Gruppe Grüner in Ternovaya failed completely. Grüner was able to receive aerial resupply from the Luftwaffe as well as numerous Ju-88 bombing missions from KG 51, which stiffened morale in his encircled command. Ryabyshev severely miscalculated when he believed

Soviet BT-7 and BT-2 tanks from the 13th Tank Brigade in 38th Army support the attack of 124th Rifle Division against Gruppe Reck's *Stützpunkt* in Peschanoe on the morning of 12 May. German defenders were amazed by the quantity of Soviet tanks thrown against them that morning, even though motley collections of obsolescent tanks such as these were quite vulnerable to 3.7cm and 5cm anti-tank guns. (Fonds of the RGKFD, Krasnogorsk)

that a single rifle division without tank support could eliminate the German garrison in Ternovaya. Instead, Ryabyshev had to settle for merely containing Grüner, which simply tied up his resources. Further north, Gordov's 21st Army continued to advance. The 227th Rifle Division and 10th Tank Brigade boldly pushed 6km west into an area where there were no German forces, while the 293rd and 76th Rifle Divisions enveloped the German 79. Infanterie-Division *Stutzpünkte* in Murom and Grafovka. A great deal of AOK 6's success in resisting the Soviet northern offensive was owed to the tenacity of the 79. Infanterie-Division, which held off 21st Army for three days without significant reinforcements. Although Gordov's troops gained ground, he made a signal mistake in not keeping pressure on the rest of XVII AK's front, which allowed Strecker to begin transferring troops from the quiet Belgorod sector to reinforce the 79. Infanterie-Division. By the end of the day, the Soviet northern group was continuing to advance westwards in the centre, but its spearheads were pushing into a salient with German counterattacks forming on both flanks and Grüner's Stützpunkt in their rear.

15 May

For the fourth day, Ryabyshev's forces continued to attack the remnants of the 294. Infanterie-Division. The 169th and 175th Rifle Division advanced another 5km and reached the outskirts of Liptsy. Ryabyshev tried to resolve the siege of Ternovaya by ordering the 38th Rifle Division to launch another attack against Gruppe Grüner, but this attack failed as well. Without substantial armour, artillery or air support, the 38th Rifle Division was not up to the task of reducing this fortified town. Gordov's 21st Army continued to advance, enveloping Gruppe Bonin at Murom and pushing back the 79. Infanterie-Division. However, the Soviet offensive was beginning to run out of steam due to the lack of sufficient reserves or second-echelon forces. The assault groups had suffered significant losses after four days of fighting and were fast reaching their culmination point, where they could no longer overpower German defences.

Meanwhile, LI AK shifted the 3. Panzer-Division northwards to strike the front of the 28th Army's advance, while the 23. Panzer-Division continued to push against the 226th Rifle Division towards Peremoga. Kampfgruppe Schmidt-Ott struck the 244th Rifle Division near Hill 205 and shattered it, with one rifle regiment and an artillery regiment overrun and about

LEFT
A platoon of Soviet T-34 tanks advancing to contact on a rising slope. Note the commanders with open hatches to increase visibility. German anti-tank guns were usually not spotted until they opened fire. (From the fonds of the RGAKFD in Krasnogorsk via Stavka)

RIGHT
German infantry observe burning T-34s in front of their position. This Soviet tank attack has come to grief before reaching the main German defensive line, probably due to 8.8cm Flak guns deployed behind the German infantry. (Ian Barter)

700 prisoners taken. Throughout most of the day, the 23. Panzer-Division fought off counterattacks by Soviet tanks around Hill 205 as Ryabyshev committed his armour piecemeal. The result was that the Panzers knocked out 16 Soviet tanks, including at least three T-34s. The only thing stopping the Panzers from fully exploiting their success was a battery of 76.2mm anti-tank guns in Rodimtsev's sector, which harassed the Panzers with accurate flanking fire. However, due to the collapse of the 244th Rifle Division, Rodimstev's 13th Guards Rifle Division was also forced backwards by the new German counterattack and his total losses were approaching 50 per cent. Consequently, two of Ryabyshev's four shock groups were disabled, bringing his offensive to a virtual standstill. With the Red steamroller stopped, LI AK then directed both Panzer divisions to attack towards Ternovaya in order to relieve Gruppe Grüner.

The first reinforcements from the Belgorod area began to arrive to reinforce the right flank of XVII AK. Infanterie-Regiment 172 from the 75. Infanterie-Division was trucked down to Liptsy, where it was just in time to stop the 169th Rifle Division from severing the main Kharkov–Belgorod road. A larger force, Gruppe Gollwitzer[4] from the 88. Infanterie-Division, arrived north-west of Murom and, by the afternoon, was beginning to attack towards the encircled German troops in Murom. By the end of the day, the northern group's offensive was degenerating into a slugging match, with the initiative rapidly shifting towards the Germans.

16 May

Recognizing that the Luftwaffe's air superiority over the Kharkov battlefield threatened the entire offensive, Timoshenko prevailed upon the Stavka for more VVS reinforcements. He was duly provided with the 220th Fighter Division (220 IAD), which arrived with two regiments of LaGG and two regiments of MiG-3 fighters. Timoshenko ordered them to regain air superiority over the 28th Army. However, the Luftwaffe continued to transfer more units back from the Crimea and these four Soviet fighter regiments failed to tip the balance. Instead, the Luftwaffe steadily increased attacks against the northern group and prevented the VVS from effectively using its own close air support.

There was less activity on the ground this day, as both sides reorganized their forces and sought to bring up reinforcements. Timoshenko had the 277th Rifle Division and 58th Tank Brigade en route from South-Western Front reserves to replenish Ryabyshev's 28th Army. The only Soviet forces still actively advancing were the 175th and 227th Rifle Divisions, each with modest tank support, into the gap north of Liptsy. Strecker's XVII AK had very few troops in this sector, where there was a 16km-wide gap between the remnants of 79. and 294. Infanterie-Divisionen. Timoshenko encouraged these kinds of advances even though they were tactically useless, since they enabled him to assure Stalin that he was still gaining ground. He spent rather less time informing Stalin about his inability to reduce Grüner's Stützpunkt in Ternovaya or the fact that most of the northern group had shifted to the defence and was being pummelled by German Panzer counterattacks that he had down-played as unlikely.

---

4 Elements included I, II, III/IR 245; I, III/IR 442; Pioneer-Abteilung 188; IV/AR 239; one armoured car squadron and one *Panzerjäger Kompanie*.

Kampfgruppe Schmidt-Ott continued to attack towards Ternovaya to relieve Gruner, but spent most of the day resupplying and fending off local Soviet counterattacks. Schmidt-Ott's Panzers destroyed five more Soviet tanks. However, Soviet anti-tank teams armed with the 14.5mm PTRD anti-tank rifle proved a significant threat by killing or wounding six German tank commanders in Panzer-Regiment 6.

17 May

After five days of attacking, the Soviet northern group had advanced no further than 15km towards Kharkov and had still failed to achieve a decisive breakthrough. Consequently, Timoshenko realized that his offensive was grinding to a halt and that he had to do something to regain the initiative or it would fail completely. Although all three of the northern group armies were badly depleted, Timoshenko gambled that AOK 6 was in even worse shape. The previous evening, he had issued Order No. 00317, directing all three armies to continue the offensive. Ryabyshev would still be the main effort since he was the closest to Kharkov, while Gordov's 21st Army would continue to support Ryabyshev by pushing towards the north-west. Moskalenko's divisions were too depleted to take on the strong German forces deployed now on the Babka line, but Timoshenko ordered him to conduct a diversionary attack against the Chugeev sector, which had been denuded of troops to rebuild the Babka line. Moskalenko demurred and asked for another day. It was an inelegant plan, with no attempt at manoeuvre – just brute force pushing towards Kharkov. However, Ryabyshev's 28th Army no longer had enough combat-effective forces left for such tactics.

Before Ryabyshev's 28th Army had even begun to move, the Germans made their main bid to relieve Gruppe Grüner in Ternovaya. At 0600hrs, the 3. and 23. Panzer-Divisionen, as well as IR 172 and IR 211, attacked the centre of Ryabyshev's front in the Murom River valley. Oberstleutnant Hermann Zimmermann's Schützen-Regiment 394 achieved great success, capturing 800 soldiers from the 244th Rifle Division near Hill 204.3. The 169th and 244th Rifle Divisions were both badly mangled,

LEFT
After the initial tank panic, the German infantry settled down and doggedly defended their fortified villages. Note that this defender has, in addition to his MG34 machine gun, his Kar 98k rifle and a captured Soviet PPSh-41 submachine gun. Even when surrounded, most German units held until relieved. (Ian Barter)

RIGHT
An 8.8cm Flak gun in action against Soviet tanks. By 23 May, the German VIII AK had been reinforced with 23 8.8cm Flak guns, which destroyed 68 Soviet tanks and thereby helped to prevent a breakthrough by 21st and 23rd Tanks Corps. (Ian Barter)

but Ryabyshev committed his last reserves – the 6th Guards Tank Brigade and the 162nd Rifle Division – to counterattack the German penetration. Beginning at 0900hrs, a swirling tank battle involving over 100 German tanks and 100-plus Soviet tanks developed around Hill 200.9. First, the Germans used artillery fire and Stuka attacks to repulse the 169th Rifle Division, which fell back. Next, 3. Panzer-Division brought up a battery of four 8.8cm Flak guns to stop the Soviet tanks. Nevertheless, 13 Panzers were total losses and the Germans were momentarily hard pressed. Gradually, the German Panzers gained the upper hand and repulsed the Soviet tankers with heavy losses. With Ryabyshev's last reserves spent, Kampfgruppe Schmidt-Ott from 3. Panzer-Division and Kampfgruppe Soltmann from 23. Panzer-Division pressed ahead and linked up with Grüner at Ternovaya in the afternoon. Soviet infantry from the 38th Rifle Division besieging Ternovaya retreated from their positions as the Panzers approached. Grüner's encircled forces had survived for five days and contributed to frustrating Ryabshev's advance on Kharkov. Due to this success, Paulus decided to detach Kampfgruppe Heydebreck (I/Pz.Rgt. 201) from 23. Panzer-Division and send it southwards during the night to support VIII AK.

Ryabyshev's centre was virtually blown out and the divisions on his flank were now vulnerable to being isolated by any further German advance. Ryabyshev was forced to commit his exploitation force, the 3rd Guards Cavalry Corps, to plug the gap. The 56th Cavalry Division moved to the centre of the line, filling the gap where the 244th Rifle Division had been. Although this ad hoc effort prevented a complete rout of 28th Army, cavalry was not intended to hold ground against Panzers and Ryabyshev had little combat-effective infantry or armour remaining. The only bright spot on the day's ledger was that Gordov's 21st Army had captured Stützpunkt Murom. Yet Gordov's three rifle divisions were now exhausted and elements of the 168. Infanterie-Division were beginning to arrive to reinforce the battered 79. Infanterie-Division.

18 May

By this point, Timoshenko realized that the northern group was not going to succeed in reaching Kharkov, but he was aware that the Germans were planning a major counteroffensive against the Barvenkovo salient and his main intent was now to prevent either the 3. or 23. Panzer-Divisionen from shifting to support that operation. Consequently, he ordered the 28th and 38th Armies to conduct limited fixing attacks to force AOK 6 to keep both Panzer divisions in this sector. However, the 23. Panzer-Division was able to dispatch Kampfgruppe Heydebreck to support the hard-pressed VIII AK. Having gained as much ground as it could hold, the 21st Army shifted to the defence.

After days of sitting out the battle, Moskalenko attacked the German infantry near Nepokrytaya at 0700hrs with the 124th and 226th Rifle Divisions, supported by 71 tanks from 13th and 36th Tank Brigades. However, the Luftwaffe was now supreme over this part of the battlefield and the Soviet shock groups were brought to an abrupt halt by relentless air attacks. After advancing less than 2km, Moskalenko broke off the attack. He also decided to abort the diversionary operation by 81st and 300th Rifle Division against Chugeev.

Around 1130 hours, Ryabyshev attacked the flank of the 23. Panzer-Division with the 38th and 162nd Rifle Divisions, as well as the fresh 277th Rifle Division, along with the remaining tanks. Barnbeck's IR 211, holding Hill 205, was pounded by Soviet artillery and then struck by small groups of tanks and infantry. German howitzers from Artillerie-Regiment 171, deployed in the open behind Hill 205, bombarded the attacking Soviets when they were outlined on the ridge. 10. Batterie of AR 171, equipped with 15cm s.FH18 howitzers, knocked out five Soviet tanks with direct fire at a range of 1,500m, which helped to break the Soviet momentum. Although the Soviet infantry was able to isolate Kampfgruppe Grüner in Ternovaya again, all other attacks were repulsed and the Luftwaffe wreaked havoc on Soviet troops in the open. In one attack at 1750hrs, StG 77 massed 32 Stukas against Soviet troops on Hill 200.9. The inability of the VVS to prevent Luftwaffe air attacks made further Soviet ground attacks in this sector pointless.

19 May

The northern group's strength was spent and it was only capable of local attacks. Ryabyshev managed to scrape up two rifle battalions and ten tanks to attack German positions south of Ternovaya around 0930hrs, but this was a futile gesture intended to appease Timoshenko. There were still about 150 tanks left with the northern group's eight tank brigades, but they were scattered and efforts to concentrate them only invited Stuka attacks. In contrast, the German Panzers in LI AK were concentrated and enjoyed complete freedom of manoeuvre.

Gordov's 21st Army was particularly exposed, with three exhausted rifle divisions trying to hold a 25km-long front with negligible armour support. Strecker's XVII AK had received part of the 168. Infanterie-Division and Kampfgruppe Gollwitzer from the 88. Infanterie-Division to take over this sector, as well as two regiments from 57. Infanterie-Division en route. Yet, when it became clear that Gordov's troops were thinly stretched, Strecker decided to counterattack with just infantry to recover Murom. Gollwitzer's counterattack sent the 293rd Rifle Division reeling and reached the outskirts of Murom. Timoshenko ordered a cavalry division and motorized rifle brigade from the 3rd Guards Cavalry Corps to plug the hole in 21st Army's lines. The 3rd Guards Cavalry Corps was now responsible for filling holes in both 21st and 28th Army lines, indicating the poverty of the northern group's resources to German intelligence officers. The Soviet position was now extremely vulnerable, with a strong German salient lodged in its centre and five divisions at risk of encirclement.

A knocked-out KV-1 heavy tank with three prominent 8.8cm penetrations on its turret and multiple smaller calibre hits on its gun mantlet. Timoshenko was provided with 80 KV-1 tanks for his offensive but split them equally between the southern and northern attack groups and then committed into combat in small platoon- and company-size detachments. (Ian Barter)

20 May

Ignoring the deteriorating front-line situation, Timoshenko issued the same unrealistic orders to the northern group as on previous days: continue attacking. He also told Ryabyshev to keep the fresh 277th Rifle Division and 58th Tank Brigade out of the attack, effectively leaving them to sit out the battle. During the night of 19/20 May, the Germans calmly repositioned 3. Panzer-Division north of Liptsy and brought up two infantry regiments from 57. Infanterie-Division to form an assault group. Timoshenko was completely ignorant of these German dispositions.

Ryabyshev ordered the 169th and 175th Rifle Divisions to continue advancing east, right towards 3. Panzer-Division. The Germans waited until the sun was overhead and then counterattacked with the three assault groups they had carefully positioned opposite the 21st and 28th Armies. The 3. Panzer-Division struck the 175th Rifle Division and routed it, then hit the flank of the 169th Rifle Division. Simultaneously, the 23. Panzer-Division hit the middle of the 28th Army, preventing 3rd Guards Cavalry Corps from moving to counter the other German penetrations. Kampfgruppe Gollwitzer achieved more success, penetrating into the outskirts of Murom by 1700hrs and forcing the 21st Army to retreat 10–15km and abandon most of its gains.

The Soviet northern group's offensive had come to an ignominious end. While the 21st and 28th Armies managed to retain some of the terrain captured since the beginning of the offensive, they had failed their primary mission of creating a breakthrough that led to the encirclement of AOK 6 in Kharkov. Once it was clear that the northern group was no longer a threat, Bock ordered Paulus to immediately pull 3. and 23. Panzer-Divisionen out of the line so that they could participate in *Fridericus*. From their initial total of 262 tanks, these two Panzer divisions only had 54 combat-ready tanks left by the end of the northern fighting, but could repair many within days. The XVII AK shifted to the defence and Strecker ordered Kampfgruppe Grüner to abandon Ternovaya since it was too difficult to hold. Three of the infantry regiments transferred from XXIX AK at Belgorod were quickly returned, demonstrating that the German philosophy of accepting risk in quiet sectors could lead to decisive results. Both sides began digging in again and attention shifted southwards.

THE SOUTHERN GROUP, 12–16 MAY 1942

Opposite General-Lieutenant Avksentiy M. Gorodniansky's 6th Army, Generaloberst Walter Heitz's VIII AK had the 62. Infanterie-Division, the 454. Sicherungs-Division and the Hungarian 108th Light Infantry Division deployed on a 75km-wide sector between Ligovka and Cherkas'kyi Bishkin. This sector had been trouble for AOK 6 since February and a new front line had only been created with great difficulty. The largest chunk of the corps' sector was held by the 454. Sicherungs-Division, which only had 6,097 men on 11 May. The security troops were equipped with elderly German and captured Soviet equipment, including 35 3.7cm Pak and 16 Russian 45mm Pak. To fight Soviet heavy tanks, the security troops were given exactly ten Stielgranate 41 rounds for their 3.7cm Pak. Heitz's strongest formation was the 62. Infanterie-Division, which had a jumbled mix of three infantry regiments from three other divisions that it had acquired during the winter fighting. These three regiments had to hold a 31km-wide sector – triple the doctrinal norm for German defensive doctrine. Nevertheless, the 62. Infanterie was at full-strength in troops and relatively well provided with anti-tank weaponry, including 12 5cm Pak, six 4.7cm Pak and 58 3.7cm Pak (with 100 Stielgranaten rounds). All told, Heitz's HKL fielded 21 infantry battalions, which was insufficient to hold the front line in any kind of strength. Since the terrain was flat and open in the VIII AK sector, Bock provided Heitz with two 8.8cm Flak guns and promised more if needed. While Heitz had no reserves of his own, the 113. Infanterie-Division and Sturmgeschütz-Abteilung 244 with 21 StuG IIIs were sitting 20km behind his corps HKL; both units had been reserved by Paulus for employment in *Fridericus*.

Unlike the Soviet northern group, which employed three armies to achieve a breakthrough, the southern group relied primarily upon Gorodniansky's 6th Army to achieve the same end. He had four rifle divisions and three tank brigades in his first echelon, followed by two rifle divisions and a tank brigade in second echelon. The 21st and 23rd Tank Corps were located 30km behind Gorodniansky, ready to exploit the breakthrough. On his left, Army Group Bobkin was deployed with three rifle divisions and a tank brigade to act as a flank guard to protect 6th Army's advance. The South-Western Front also had the 2nd Cavalry Corps and two rifle divisions in reserve within a day's march of 6th Army. It was clear that Timoshenko lavished far more resources in developing the

Noskov's 6th Cavalry Corps was committed into the breach created by Army Group Bobkin and advanced rapidly towards Krasnograd. However, the lightly armed cavalry units could not fight their way into the city, even against weak resistance. (Courtesy of the Central Museum of the Armed Forces, Moscow, via Stavka)

The attack of 6th Army and Army Group Bobkin, 12–18 May 1942

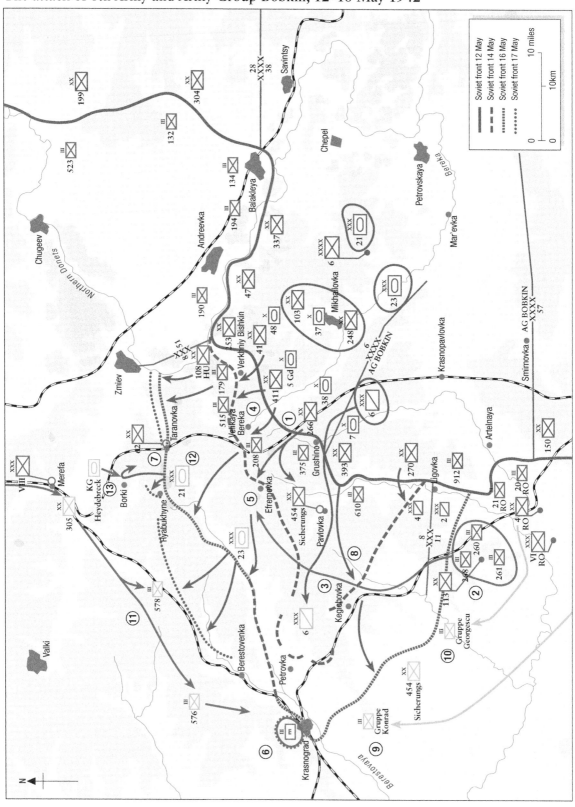

1. 12 May, 6th Army attacks with its main effort directed at the boundary between the 62. Infanterie-Division and the 454. Sicherungs-Division, creating a small breach in the VIII AK front.
2. 12–13 May, the Germans rapidly commit the 113. Infanterie-Division to seal the breach by creating a new line at Efremovka.
3. 13 May, Army Group Bobkin pushes Noskov's 6th Cavalry Corps towards the Orel River.
4. 13–14 May, the 6th Army fights its way through the 62. Infanterie-Division's line between Verkhniy Bishkin and Velikaya Bereka.
5. 13–14 May, heavy fighting around Efremovka as the left wing of 6th Army tries to bash its way through the 113. Infanterie-Division's line.
6. 14 May, Sperrverband Ziegelmayer formed to hold Krasnograd.
7. 15 May, VIII AK falls back to a new line.
8. 15 May, Army Group Bobkin continues to push back 454. Sicherungs-Division.
9. 16 May, Gruppe Konrad moves into gap south of Krasnograd to block Army Group Bobkin's advance.
10. 16 May, Gruppe Georgescu from Romanian 4th Division bolsters 454. Sicherungs-Division flank.
11. 17 May, 305. Infanterie-Division arrives in sector, with IR 576 proceeding to Krasnograd and IR 578 to defend the Krasnograd Kharkov railway line.
12. 17 May, the 21st and 23rd Tank Corps are committed into battle, straining VIII AK's defences.
13. 18 May, fighting around Borki and Ryabukhyne contains 21st Tank Corps. Kampfgruppe Heydebreck arrives and counterattacks at Borki.

southern assault group compared to the northern group, which lacked adequate reserves or an exploitation force. However, Timoshenko put little effort into planning for the Southern Front's 9th and 57th Armies occupying the southern part of the Barvenkovo salient and allowed them to slide into a passive defensive mindset.

12 May

Gorodniansky's artillery preparation began at 0630hrs, synchronized with the northern group's bombardment. Some 485 artillery pieces pounded the German front-line positions, including 117 122mm and 127 152mm howitzers and an MRL battalion. At 0730hrs, Gorodniansky began his ground attack, with four rifle divisions and three tank brigades (124 tanks) advancing on a 26km-wide front. Overhead, the VVS provided 34 Il-2 Sturmoviks and 19 Pe-2 bombers for air support to 6th Army, but due to a planning error none went to Army Group Bobkin. On the 6th Army's right flank, the 253rd and 41st Rifle Divisions conducted limited fixing attacks without armour support against the Hungarian 108th Light Division and IR 179 in Stützpunkt Verkhniy Bishkin. Gorodniansky made his main effort on his left flank against the boundary between the 62. Infanterie-Division and 454. Sicherungs-Division. The 411th Rifle Division, supported by 40 tanks of the 48th Tank Brigade, attacked straight into the centre of the 62. Infanterie-Division's sector and enveloped part of IR 208. The 266th Rifle Division, supported by 80 tanks of the 38th and 5th Guards Tank Brigades, attacked Major Richard Wolf's IR 208 directly and managed to encircle Major Karl Jurisch's II/IR 208 south of Velikaya Bereka and overrun two artillery batteries. German artillery managed to prevent a complete

LEFT
Once the Soviet armies began moving forward, older division-level artillery pieces like this M1910/37 152mm howitzer had difficulty keeping up. The Red Army still employed a number of howitzers from World War I and they were clearly outclassed by German division-level weapons like the 10.5cm l.FH18. (Nik Cornish at Stavka)

RIGHT
German artillery forward observer positions like this one, concealed in tall grass, were difficult to detect and they enabled the Germans to call down destructive fire on Soviet troop concentrations in the open. (Nik Cornish at Stavka)

collapse by sacrificing a number of guns in direct-fire mode, but could only delay the Soviet shock groups. By 1300hrs, the right flank of 62. Infanterie-Division was in serious trouble as IR 208's positions were smashed by the red hammer of tanks, artillery and a 9:1 superiority in infantry. One infantry battalion was transferred from IR 179's sector to reinforce the faltering IR 208, briefly stabilizing the situation. Nevertheless, in exchange for the loss of 12 tanks and some infantry, the 6th Army had advanced 6–8km.

Army Group Bobkin conducted a supporting attack with the 393rd Rifle Division and 7th Tank Brigade (40 tanks) against IR 375 of the 454. Sicherungs-Division at Gruschino. By 1000hrs, the security troops were put to flight by the Soviet tanks, falling back 4–6km. This area was a weak point in the VIII AK front and Bobkin was quick to realize the potential to expand his supporting attack into a real breakthrough. He duly brought up General-Major Aleksandr A. Noskov's 6th Cavalry Corps and committed it into the breakthrough corridor before evening. Although the official Soviet history later claimed that 6th Army 'shattered German resistance along a 42km front', this was nonsense since both the 62. Infanterie-Division and 454. Sicherungs-Division were still limiting the Soviet southern group to minor advances. In fact, the 454. Sicherungs-Division had only been struck a glancing blow on its two left flank battalions, causing it to refuse its flank and form a new line behind the Orel River.

The opening day of the Soviet offensive revealed serious mistakes in Soviet planning. First, the Southern Front had not been properly brought into the planning process, which meant forces that could have supported the offensive were left idle. Second, Soviet intelligence somehow missed the presence of the 113. Infanterie-Division sitting in reserve just behind 6th Army's intended breakthrough sector. This division was put on alert immediately after the Soviet artillery preparation began and was subordinated to VIII AK. Heitz ordered it to send IR 260 and an artillery battalion to seal the narrow breach created by Bobkin's troops. Paulus also decided to detach Panzerjäger-Abteilung 128 from 23. Panzer-Division and send it to reinforce Heitz as well.

13 May

By the second morning of the offensive, it was clear that Gorodniansky's 6th Army had not achieved a clean breakthrough against the 62. Infanterie-Division, but had created a dangerous gap between it and the 454. Sicherungs-Division. The town of Efremovka was in this area and the 266th Rifle Division and 38th Tank Brigade headed straight for it. However, the 113. Infanterie-Division was hastily moved up in an effort to seal the breach and its IR 261 and a company of assault guns reached Efremovka first, establishing a defensive line along the Orel River. IR 260 fell in on its right flank. When the Soviet vanguard reached the river, the 113. Infanterie-Division mounted a five-battalion counterattack across the river, which momentarily halted the 266th Rifle Division. Later in the evening, the 266th Rifle Division conducted a rare night attack by fording the river with a rifle regiment and a few tanks, which then attacked into Efremovka. German infantry from IR 261 and the assault guns of Sturmgeschütz-Abteilung 244 repulsed the attack.

As for the 62. Infanterie-Division, its IR 179 still held solidly onto Stützpunkt Verkhniy Bishkin but its left flank was hard pressed by 1400 hrs. Major Jurisch's II/IR 208 was surrounded and the remainder of IR 208 reduced to a battalion-size *Kampfgruppe*. In order to prevent a collapse,

Heitz transferred two Hungarian infantry battalions from their relatively quiet sector to reinforce the 62. Infanterie-Division's right flank. Soviet air support was already evaporating as Timoshenko made the disastrous decision to pull air units from the south to support the northern group offensive. Even without air support, the 6th Army had enough tanks and artillery to overrun the 62. Infanterie-Division's battalion-size *Stutzpünkte* but, instead, Gorodniansky chose to envelop them. While the 253rd Rifle Division gradually slipped around the flanks of Verkhniy Bishkin, the 41st and 411th Rifle Divisions began to envelop IR 515's positions. The result was that 6th Army wasted virtually an entire day trying to maneuver around 62. Infanterie-Division, rather than crushing it. Soviet claims that the 62. Infanterie-Division and the Hungarians were routed were patently false.

Bobkin's limited offensive gained more momentum until Noskov's cavalry ran into Aufklärungs-Abteilung 113 (Reconnaissance Battalion) near the Orel River. The 393rd Rifle Division was still working to enlarge its breakthrough in this sector – in fact, the only actual breakthrough achieved by the southern group. Noskov's three cavalry divisions, with a total of about 18,000 troopers, filed through the narrow penetration corridor and headed west towards Krasnograd. However, Bobkin started with only 40 tanks and a limited amount of infantry, most of which was focused on holding open and enlarging the corridor, meaning virtually nothing was left to support Noskov's deep exploitation operation. At this point, with 6th Army hung up on a series of German strongpoints and Bobkin advancing into a gap in the German line, Timoshenko should have released the 21st and 23rd Tank Corps to Bobkin, but he deferred. Timoshenko decided to await committing the two tanks corps until Gorodniansky achieved greater success. He regarded Bobkin's role as still secondary and was not willing to modify his plan to accommodate ground truth.

Meanwhile, the hard-pressed German infantry in VIII Armeekorps were trading space for time, using delaying tactics instead of adopting a 'die-in-place' mindset with each *Stützpunkt*. Thanks to a weak Soviet pursuit effort, German rearguards were usually able to keep falling back to secondary positions, although the artillery and *Panzerjäger* often had to abandon heavy weapons. Bock was

A German s.FH18 15cm howitzer is ready to fire. This was the standard heavy howitzer available to support the German infantry divisions, but it was outclassed in range and performance by Soviet weapons such as the ML-20. (Ian Barter)

TO THE GREEN STEPPES BEYOND, NOSKOV'S CAVALRY, 14 MAY 1942 (PP. 60–61)

The Red Army committed 12 cavalry divisions to the Kharkov offensive and Timoshenko eagerly anticipated their ability to advance westwards across the steppe country once the infantry and tanks had broken through AOK 6's thinly manned front line. One of the more hapless units caught in the path of Army Group Bobkin was the 454. Sicherungs-Division, normally employed in rear-area anti-partisan operations but forced into front-line service due to the shortage of German infantry after the heavy losses of 1941. On the left flank of 454. Sicherungs-Division was its best unit, the two-battalion Infanterie-Regiment 375, which held defensive positions near the town of Grushino. Bobkin's infantry quickly overwhelmed the German defences near

Grushino, forcing IR 375 to retreat to the south-west. Once a breakthrough was achieved, Bobkin committed Noskov's 6th Cavalry Corps into the breach and ordered them to advance rapidly towards the west. Noskov's cavalry conducted a mounted advance with three divisions on line, supported by the 7th Tank Brigade. Along the way to Krasnograd, Noskov's cavalry encountered retreating German elements and occasional knots of resistance. Here, troopers from the 137th Cavalry Regiment **(1)** catch up with a retreating column from IR 375 and, after a brief firefight, capture the group **(2)**. A BT-7 from 7th Tank Brigade **(3)** is one of the few tanks that can keep up with the fast-moving Soviet cavalry.

unsure if the best method of countering the Soviet breakthrough was to order Kleist to execute *Fridericus* as soon as possible or to send one Panzer division and some infantry to conduct a local counterattack in support of VIII Armeekorps. However, Bock was a cautious commander and did not believe that Kleist had sufficient forces to achieve a 'big solution' by cutting off the Barvenkovo salient without help from AOK 6, and he leaned towards the 'small solution' of just stopping Army Group Bobkin's drive on Krasnograd. Despite Bock's uncertainty, once it became clear that the Southern Front was not participating in Timoshenko's offensive, Kleist began redeploying his Panzers and motorized infantry to assembly areas opposite the 9th Army in order to be prepared to execute *Fridericus* on schedule. If Heitz's infantry could hold off the southern group long enough, Kleist believed that he would be able to deliver a powerful counterthrust that could put all the Soviet forces in the Barvenkovo salient in jeopardy.

14 May

Stopped dead by the 62. Infanterie-Division *Stutzpünkte*-anchored HKL, the 6th Army conducted an all-out attack with the 253rd, 41st and 411th Rifle Divisions against the fortified villages of Verkhniy Bishkin and Velikaya Bereka. Although Gorodniansky's troops received negligible air support, they had plenty of artillery and tank support. Three KV-1 tanks overran one position west of the rail line, crushing the German Pak guns underneath their tracks. As a result, the division was reduced to only two operational 5cm Pak guns. Nevertheless, the 62. Infanterie-Division held its ground for most of the day, inflicting significant losses on the attacking Soviet tanks and infantry, while the Luftwaffe provided some Stuka support, which bolstered the morale of the German infantry. As dusk approached, the 62. Infanterie-Division fell back 4–5km and dug in on a new line south of Taranovka. Once again, the Soviets failed to energetically pursue the Germans, enabling them to conduct an orderly retreat. After burying his heavy weapons and radios, Major Jurisch led his encircled II/IR 208 in a breakout through the Soviet lines during the night and marched 7km to reach friendly positions. There was no doubt that Heitz's VIII Armeekorps was hard pressed, but the ability of the 62. Infanterie-Division to conduct a fighting withdrawal against vastly superior enemy forces for three days gave time for vital German reinforcements to get in the fight. In the afternoon, Bock received an order from Hitler to execute *Fridericus* with Kleist's Panzers as soon as possible.

On the left flank of 6th Army, the 266th Rifle Division and 38th Tank Brigade encountered two regiments of the 113. Infanterie-Division dug in near Efremovka. The Sturmgeschütz-Abteilung 244 acted as a mobile fire brigade in this sector and knocked out 12 Matilda tanks at the cost of nine of its 21 StuG-IIIs. Army Group Bobkin's 6th Cavalry Corps continued to advance towards Krasnograd and Paulus decided to form a blocking unit from whatever was available in the vicinity. Oberstleutnant Karl Ziegelmeyer, commander of Heeres-Pionier-Bataillon 260, was ordered to form Sperrverband Ziegelmayer and prevent Noskov's cavalry from seizing the city in a *coup de main*. Initially, Ziegelmayer had fewer than 600 engineers and construction troops, but he rapidly established a screen line east of the city while gathering up other rear-echelon troops. The 305. Infanterie-Division had begun arriving in Kharkov from France and Paulus decided to split the unit up, with IR 576 heading to Krasnograd and the rest of the division going to fill the yawning gap between Krasnograd and the 113. Infanterie-Division's

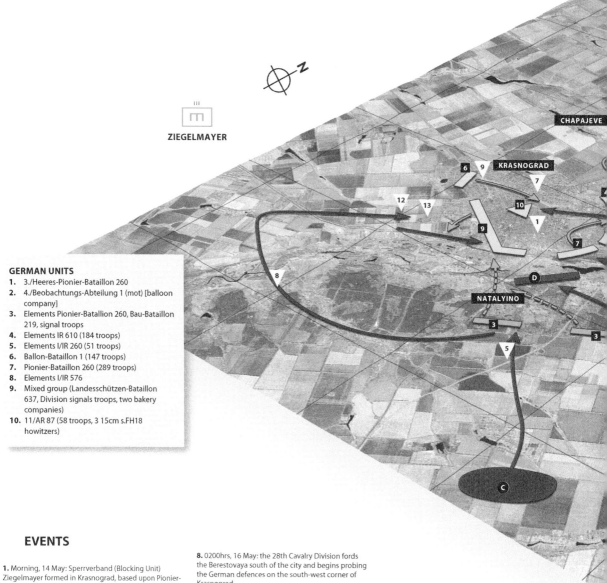

ZIEGELMAYER

GERMAN UNITS
1. 3./Heeres-Pionier-Bataillon 260
2. 4./Beobachtungs-Abteilung 1 (mot) [balloon company]
3. Elements Pionier-Bataillon 260, Bau-Bataillon 219, signal troops
4. Elements IR 610 (184 troops)
5. Elements I/IR 260 (51 troops)
6. Ballon-Bataillon 1 (147 troops)
7. Pionier-Bataillon 260 (289 troops)
8. Elements I/IR 576
9. Mixed group (Landesschützen-Bataillon 637, Division signals troops, two bakery companies)
10. 11/AR 87 (58 troops, 3 15cm s.FH18 howitzers)

EVENTS

1. Morning, 14 May: Sperrverband (Blocking Unit) Ziegelmayer formed in Krasnograd, based upon Pionier-Bataillon 260 and Bau-Bataillon 219 (Construction battalion). More units join over next two days.

2. Afternoon, 14 May: Ziegelmayer establishes a screen line between Natalyino and Zigerovka.

3. 2400hrs, 14 May: Soviet cavalry pushes back screening units at Balki and Zigerovka.

4. 0110–1030hrs, 15 May: demolition squads from Pionier-Bataillon 260 begin blowing up bridges over Berestovaya River.

5. 0700–1100hrs, 15 May: all three Soviet cavalry divisions attack Ziegelmayer's screen line in force and force the German units to evacuate the eastern bank.

6. 1630–2300hrs, 15 May: the 49th Cavalry Division fords the Berestovaya north-east of Krasnograd.

7. 0200hrs, 16 May: two battalions from 49th Cavalry Division suddenly attack and overrun the detachment from IR 610. Soviet cavalry fight their way into the north-east corner of the city and nearly overrun the 15cm howitzer battery.

8. 0200hrs, 16 May: the 28th Cavalry Division fords the Berestovaya south of the city and begins probing the German defences on the south-west corner of Krasnograd.

9. 0845–0900hrs, 16 May: German counterattack, including troops from Ballon-Bataillon 1 and Stuka support, eject the Soviet cavalry from the northern corner of Krasnograd and restore the defensive line.

10. Evening, 16 May: lead elements of IR 576 arrive and take over defence of northern sector, enabling Ziegelmayer to regroup his forces to reinforce the south.

11. 0130hrs, 18 May: after regrouping on 17 May, the 49th Cavalry Division fords the river at Lipianka and manages to its way into the eastern suburbs, but is stopped cold.

12. Evening, 18 May: the 28th Cavalry Division attacks the south-west corner of the city and captures a large collective farm on the outskirts.

13. 1500–1800hrs, 19 May: a German counterattack retakes the collective farm with difficulty, but it is clear that Noskov's cavalry lack the strength to fight their way into the city.

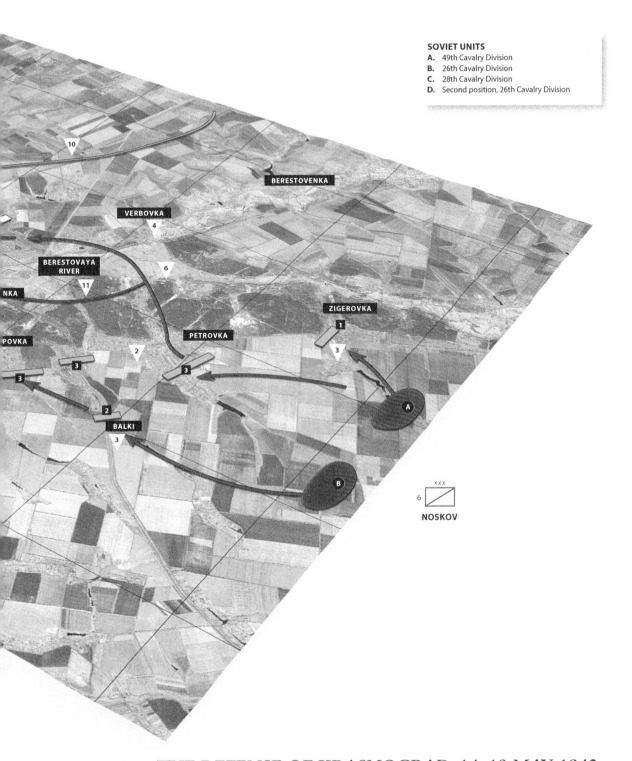

BERESTOVENKA

VERBOVKA

BERESTOVAYA
RIVER

NKA

ZIGEROVKA

PETROVKA

POVKA

BALKI

A

B

NOSKOV

THE DEFENSE OF KRASNOGRAD, 14–19 MAY 1942

Sperrverband Ziegelmayer, an ad hoc grouping of rear-echelon troops, prevents Noskov's 6th Cavalry Corps from seizing Krasnograd in a *coup de main* and fights off continuous attacks for nearly a week on its own.

65

open right flank. Two of Bobkin's other divisions, the 270th and 393rd Rifle Divisions, pushed back the left flank of the 454. Sicherungs-Division, in order to widen the penetration. Yet, despite the fact that Bobkin had the only real breakthrough in his sector, Timoshenko still deferred on committing his tank corps or second-echelon infantry. Instead, these units that might have been committed to seal the Soviet victory were left 20–40km behind the advancing spearhead units of the first-echelon. When Timoshenko updated Stalin on the operation, he stated that the southern group was progressing well, which not only was inaccurate but served to feed Stalin's optimism. In order to retain his political capital with Stalin, Timoshenko preferred to gloss over problems that he knew that the dictator did not want to hear.

15 May

By the fourth day of the Soviet offensive, Heitz was forced to give ground and ordered both the 62. and 113. Infanterie-Divisionen to fall back about 10km. The 62. Infanterie-Division established a new line just south of Taranovka, while the Hungarian 108th Light Division guarded the narrow sector between Taranovka and the Donets. The Luftwaffe committed four bomber *Gruppen* and numerous Stuka sorties to slow the Soviet pursuit and attack concentrations of tanks. The 6th Army's 253rd, 41st and 411th Rifle Divisions pursued slowly, allowing the Germans time to dig in. On the 6th Army's left flank, the 266th Rifle Division occupied Efremovka, but the 113. Infanterie-Division was able to fall back without difficulty to the Berestovaiga River, where it established a new defensive line. German pioneers efficiently destroyed all the bridges across the river, which made it difficult for 6th Army to employ its remaining tanks. The 411th Rifle Division was able to gain a toehold across the river at Okhochae before a rapid counterattack by the 113. Infanterie-Division drove them back. Army Group Bobkin also continued advancing and Noskov's cavalry quickly pushed back Sperrverband Ziegelmayer's thin security line. Ziegelmayer's engineers managed to blow up all five bridges across the Berestovaya River in the Krasnograd sector, but Noskov immediately ordered two of his cavalry divisions to seek fords north and south of the city. Owing to the destruction of the bridges, rail traffic along the Kharkov–Dnepropetrovsk line ceased. Meanwhile, Bobkin's 270th and 393rd Rifle Divisions continued to press back the 454. Sicherungs-Division and the Romanian 4th Infantry Division, causing a 35km gap between the German VIII and XI AK.

Timoshenko had his breakthrough, but he could not see it. Instead, he fretted that 6th Army was merely shoving the Germans back 4–5km each day, but without encircling or destroying any units. Armeeoberkommando 6 was simply trading space for time, which was working against Timoshenko. He decided to move up the two tanks corps a bit to keep pace with the battle, but still deferred on a decision to commit them. Given the huge gap in the German front south of Krasnograd, Timoshenko's rigid adherence to a plan that was clearly no longer relevant and his timidity in deciding when and where to commit his *masse de manoeuvre* were fatal mistakes in battle command.

The dead crew of a German 3.7cm Pak. Most *Panzerjäger* companies were still equipped with this weapon and they suffered catastrophic losses when forced to fight Soviet heavy or medium tanks, which were impervious to their standard armour-piercing rounds. (Author)

On the other side of the hill, Bock was still concerned that VIII AK would break before *Fridericus* could have any effect on Timoshenko's offensive. He was aware that Timoshenko had not yet committed his main armoured reserve and dreaded its appearance at any moment. Bock also believed that holding Krasnograd was critical, since the main rail line from Dnepropetrovsk to Kharkov lay just east of the city. If Sperrverband Ziegelmayer could not hold the city alone for several days – which seemed dubious – AOK 6's entire right flank could crumble beyond repair. After much discussion with Kleist, Bock decided to stay on course with preparations for *Fridericus* but directed XI AK to provide troops to help close the gap created by Army Group Bobkin. As a result, Gruppe Konrad was formed from one regiment of the 298. Infanterie-Division and part of the Romanian 4th Infantry Division and ordered to occupy the 35km gap between the VIII and XI AK before attacking Bobkin's left flank – a very tall order for a coalition force of less than 4,000 troops. The XI AK also formed Gruppe Georgescu, another mixed German-Romanian brigade-size force, to bolster the 454. Sicherungs-Division, which was near collapse.

16 May

The southern group's offense was brought to a virtual standstill by the VIII AK defence, which was failing gracefully rather than catastrophically as Timoshenko had planned. In particular, the 113. Infanterie-Division played a critical role in stabilizing the German front along the Berestovaya River for two days. Bock also managed to provide 14 8.8cm Flak to stiffen the corps' anti-tank defences. All four Soviet first-echelon rifle divisions were still engaged – without relief after five days of fighting. More than half of 6th Army's tanks were out of action and Soviet artillery was low on ammunition. Nevertheless, Gorodniansky stubbornly continued to attack northwards and switched to hit the Hungarian 108th Light Infantry Division, which had a momentary episode of 'tank panic' when struck by a brigade of tanks. The arrival of substantial Luftwaffe air support enabled daily Stuka attacks on concentrations of Soviet tanks and infantry also took its toll.

Yet Bobkin was still enjoying success, with Noskov's cavalry managing to ford the Berestovaya River both north and south of the city. The 49th Cavalry Division quietly approached the north-eastern sector of Krasnograd around 0445hrs and overran an infantry company and some artillery. Soviet cavalry were soon rushing into the unprotected heart of the city, forcing Ziegelmayer to organize an unlikely counterattack force that included engineers, troops from a balloon battalion, signal troops and bakers, supported by his three

A Soviet BT-7 tank burns after being knocked out. This tank probably belonged to one of the tank brigades in Moskalenko's 38th Army, which suffered heavy losses from the counterattack by the 3. and 23. Panzer-Divisionen on 13–14 May. (Author)

15cm howitzers. Amazingly, the German counterattack succeeded and restored the city's perimeter defence. Noskov had about 15,000 troops versus Ziegelmayer's 1,626 troops, but the Russian cavalry lacked the heavy artillery required to demolish the stout German-occupied buildings. By evening, the lead elements of IR 576 marched into the city, allowing Ziegelmayer to strengthen his defences on the south-west side of Krasnograd.

Gruppe Konrad had moved into the gap south of Krasnograd and was quickly engaged by two regiments of the 393rd Rifle Division. When Timoshenko noticed Germans and Romanian troops from XI AK being transferred to this area, he finally ordered the Southern Front to get into the fight with its 57th Army by attacking the thinly spread Romanian 6th Corps. Timoshenko hoped that the 57th Army could penetrate the Romanian lines, thereby precipitating a general Axis collapse between Krasnograd and Pavlograd. General-Lieutenant Kuzma P. Podlas duly carried out the order by conducting a regimental-size attack by the 150th Rifle Division against the Romanian 1st Infantry Division, but the Romanians easily repulsed the attack. This pathetic effort, lacking substantial tank or artillery support, was the maximum effort put forth by the Southern Front in support of Timoshenko's offensive.

Timoshenko knew that Kleist was gathering forces for a counteroffensive against the Barvenkovo salient and that the Soviet tank corps needed to be committed now, if they were to have a decisive affect. Yet when Timoshenko finally gave the order for both the 21st and 23rd Tank Corps to join the battle, the execution proved difficult. Gordianansky's infantry did not have a viable bridgehead across the Berestovaia River until late afternoon and it would require hours to move large armoured formations across. Consequently, Gordianansky decided not to commit the tanks corps until the next morning. Thus, five days into the offensive, the southern group had yet to introduce either its second-echelon or exploitation forces into the battle.

THE GERMAN COUNTEROFFENSIVE, 17–23 MAY 1942

'It's all or nothing here now!'

Generalfeldmarschall Fedor von Bock

While Timoshenko's northern and southern groups assaulted Paulus' AOK 6, Malinovsky's Southern Front's 57th and 9th Armies defended the 176km-long front along the southern side of the Barvenkovo salient. General-Lieutenant Kuzma P. Podlas' 57th Army had four rifle divisions defending the south-west corner of the salient, with the 14th Guards Rifle Division in reserve. Due to the inactivity of the 57th Army, the XI AK had been able to detach Gruppe Konrad to contain Army Group Bobkin south of Krasnograd. General-Major Fedor M. Kharitonov's 9th Army had six rifle divisions, two tank brigades and two anti-tank regiments (with 31 anti-tank guns) to hold the southern flank of the Barvenkovo salient and Southern Front had General-Major Issa A. Pliev's 5th Cavalry Corps in reserve behind the 9th Army. Rather than supporting Timoshenko's offensive, Kharitonov had focused most of his attention and best units on reducing a minor German position at Maiaki, just north of Slavyansk. Both Soviet armies were over-stretched, with their front-line rifle divisions averaging 20km of front, which was more than double the frontage recommended by Soviet doctrine. Even worse, Soviet intelligence completely missed the redeployment of Kleist's forces in preparation for *Fridericus*.

In the area around Stepanovka, some 30km south of Barvenkovo, Mackensen's III AK (mot.) had been assembling for four days, in anticipation of the onset of *Fridericus*. Mackensen had four divisions, including the 14. Panzer-Division with 102 tanks, the 60. Infanterie-Division (mot.) with 14 Marder IIs, 1. Gebirgs-Division, 100. leichte Infanterie-Division and Sturmgeschütz-Abteilung 245. Mackensen also had the Italian

LEFT
A Soviet fighter goes down in flames. Once the Luftwaffe units began returning from the Crimea, the Germans quickly regained air superiority around Kharkov and inflicted grievous losses upon the VVS squadrons supporting Timoshenko's offensive. (Nik Cornish at Stavka)

RIGHT
Once the Luftwaffe fighters gained air superiority around Kharkov, Ju-87 Stuka dive bombers from StG 77 wreaked havoc upon Timoshenko's ground forces, particularly during the battle for the Barvenkovo salient. (Nik Cornish at Stavka)

Group Barbo,[5] which he assigned to protect his left flank and tie in with the Romanian 6th Corps. A large stockpile of fuel and ammunition had been placed near the railhead at Krasnoarmiis'k to support the offensive. Further to the east near Slavyansk, General der Artillerie Maximilian de Angelis assembled an assault group from XXXXIV AK that included 16. Panzer-Division with 97 tanks, 97. leichte Infanterie-Division, 68, 384 and 389. Infanterie-Divisionen. In addition, LII AK provided the 101. leichte Infanterie-Division and 257. Infanterie-Division, along with some of its artillery. Kleist intended to use III AK (mot.) and XXXXIV AK to create a penetration corridor in their sectors, smash 9th Army in the process and then push rapidly towards Izyum.

17 MAY

Fridericus kicked off at 0500hrs, with over 300 artillery pieces from III and XXXXIV AK laying down a well-planned artillery preparation on the 9th Army's 51st and 106th Rifle Divisions. Once it grew light, the Luftwaffe proceeded to launch a devastating series of attacks on 9th Army's rear areas. One raid destroyed the 9th Army forward command post, which completely disrupted wire communications with all of its front-line divisions. At 0630hrs, Kleist commenced his ground attack. Mackensen's III AK punched easily through the boundary between the 341st and 106th Rifle Divisions with Generalmajor Friedrich Kühn's 14. Panzer-Division. Mackensen advanced on a three division front, with 1. Gebirgs-Division on his left, Kühn's Panzers in the middle and 100. leichte Infanterie-Division on the right. He kept the 60. Infanterie-Division (mot.) in reserve, ready to reinforce success or deal with Soviet counterattacks. Lacking effective tank or air support, the two right-flank rifle divisions of 9th Army quickly wilted under the carefully staged German combined arms attack and Mackensen tore a 20km-wide hole in Kharitonov's front. Kühn's Panzers wasted little time and rapidly advanced 18km to the outskirts of Barvenkovo, which was captured at 1700hrs.

Further east, Angelis' XXXXIV AK attacked along a wider front, with the 384. Infanterie-Division on his left, Generalleutnant Hans-Valentine Hube's 16. Panzer-Division as his spearhead and the 97. and 101. leichte Infanterie-Divisionen on his right. The 68. and 257. Infanterie-Divisionen also provided supporting attacks, while Angelis kept most of 389. Infanterie-Division in reserve. The Soviet 51st and 335th Rifle Divisions were blasted to shreds and

---

5   Equivalent to two dismounted cavalry squadrons and some armoured cars.

German infantry advance cautiously behind a StuG III assault gun. There were only two assault gun battalions involved in the campaign, one with VIII AK and the other with Mackensen's III Armeekorps (mot.). (Ian Barter)

overrun in a matter of hours, enabling Hube's Panzers to advance directly towards Kharitonov's headquarters at Kamenka, south of Izyum. Due to the collapse of communications throughout 9th Army, Kharitonov had little idea that his front-line units were being demolished and he was slow to commit his reserve units. He was also slow to inform either Malinovsky or Timoshenko about the extent of the German breakthrough. By the time that he did decide to act, the Germans had already shattered virtually his entire front and pocketed parts of the 106th, 335th and 349th Rifle Divisions. Late in the day, Kharitonov tried to fling Pliev's 5th Cavalry Corps and the 15th Tank Brigade in front of XXXXIV AK's advance, which did slow Hube down but also resulted in very heavy Soviet losses. Trying to stop a Panzer *Schwerpunkt* with cavalry was an act of desperation and, by the end of the day, Pliev's corps was fragmented and only partially combat effective. For Kleist's troops, it was like the good old days of 1941, with Soviet units paralyzed by fear and lack of command control while fast-moving Panzer units ran rings around them. Only eight of Kleist's 199 tanks were destroyed on the first day of the counteroffensive.

General-Lieutenant Kuzma P. Podlas' 57th Army was not affected immediately by the German attack and he had very little idea what was going on his left flank. His reserve unit, the 14th Guards Rifle Division, was in a good position to shift to counterattack into the flank of Mackensen's III AK, but sat idle all day. Instead, Podlas merely ordered his 351st Rifle Division to refuse its left flank to cover the gap created by Mackensen's breakthrough and assumed that Kharitonov would contain the German attack with his own resources. Since Timoshenko did not learn about the virtual collapse of 9th Army until that evening, he neither ordered any South-Western Front reserves to assist Kharitonov nor suspended the southern group's advance westwards.

A German infantry squad advancing during the early stages of the counteroffensive. The entrenching tool on the squad leader suggests that the unit will soon dig in its MG34 machine gun once it reaches a new position. (Ian Barter)

Kleist's attack, 17–22 May 1942

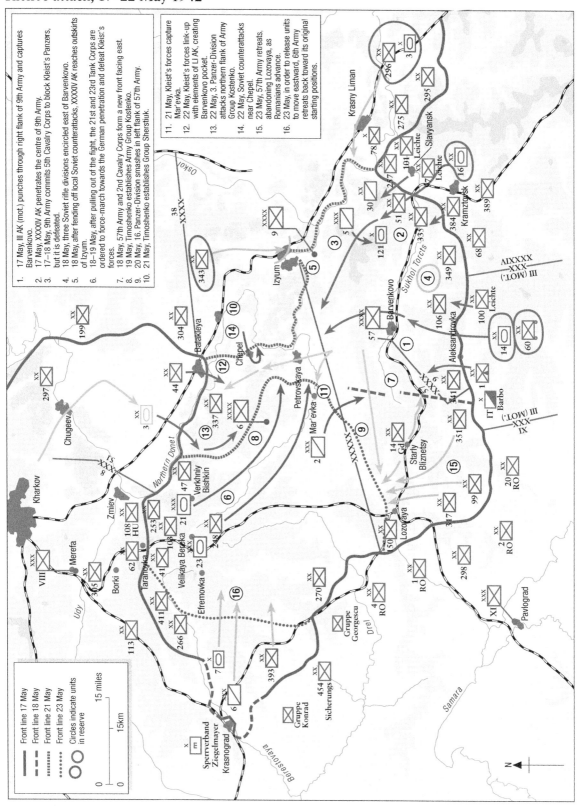

1. 17 May, III AK (mot.) punches through right flank of 9th Army and captures Barvenkovo.
2. 17 May, XXXIV AK penetrates the centre of 9th Army.
3. 17–18 May, 9th Army commits 5th Cavalry Corps to block Kleist's Panzers, but it is defeated.
4. 18 May, three Soviet rifle divisions encircled east of Barvenkovo.
5. 18 May, after fending off local Soviet counterattacks, XXXIV AK reaches outskirts of Izyum.
6. 18–19 May, after pulling out of the fight, the 21st and 23rd Tank Corps are ordered to force-march towards the German penetration and defeat Kleist's forces.
7. 18 May, 57th Army and 2nd Cavalry Corps form a new front facing east.
8. 19 May, Timoshenko establishes Army Group Kostenko.
9. 20 May, 16. Panzer-Division smashes in left flank of 57th Army.
10. 21 May, Timoshenko establishes Group Sherstiuk.
11. 21 May, Kleist's forces capture Mar'evka.
12. 22 May, Kleist's forces link-up with elements of LI AK, creating Barvenkovo pocket.
13. 22 May, 3. Panzer-Division attacks northern flank of Army Group Kostenko.
14. 22 May, Soviet counterattacks near Chepel.
15. 23 May, 57th Army retreats, abandoning Lozovaya, as Romanians advance.
16. 23 May, in order to release units to move eastward, 6th Army retreats back toward its original starting positions.

It had been a very good day for Gorodniansky's 6th Army, which finally managed to repair three bridges over the Berestovaiya River, meeting Timoshenko's requirement to commit the 21st and 23rd Tank Corps. General-Major Grigoriy I. Kuzmin's 21st Tank Corps attacked the boundary between the 62. Infanterie-Division and 113. Infanterie-Division south of Ryabukhyne, with his main effort falling on II and III/IR 261. Unable to stem the concentrated attack of 100 Soviet tanks, the two German battalions retreated back into Ryabukhyne and conducted a dogged defence, aided by three StuG IIIs and a Flak battery, that claimed 34 of Kuzmin's tanks. Lacking effective infantry support, Kuzmin decided to screen IR 261 in Ryabukhyne while pushing north towards Borki with a single brigade. With Soviet tanks behind their right flank and continued pressure from 6th Army, the 62. Infanterie-Division was forced to withdraw about 6km, abandoning most of Taranovka to Gorodniansky. The Hungarian 108th Light Infantry Division fell back to the outskirts of Zmiev. General-Major Efim G. Pushkin's 23rd Tank Corps attacked the right flank of the 113. Infanterie-Division and managed to advance westwards 15km at the cost of nine tanks. Lead elements of the 305. Infanterie-Division arrived in time to limit his advance. Army Group Bobkin had a less eventful day, with Noskov's 6th Cavalry Corps completely stymied by Ziegelmayer's hedgehog defence of Krasnograd. Bobkin's troops were also running short of ammunition, since they had not been provided with sufficient supplies for a protracted offensive.

From Timoshenko's point of view, 6th Army's offensive was on the verge of decisive victory, which would probably help to overshadow the failure of the northern group's offensive. Timoshenko was concerned about the situation in 9th Army, but still believed that Malinovsky's forces could deal with any German local success while he reaped the laurels of success achieved by the southern group. As reports from Kharitonov trickled in, Timoshenko hesitated but finally telephoned Moscow in order to inform the Stavka about the German counteroffensive. Vasilevsky immediately saw that the Germans intended to sever the Barvenkovo salient and recommended stopping the 6th Army's offensive in order to dispatch all reserves to deal with Kleist. However, Stalin did not see it that way. Instead he inflicted a useless compromise on Timoshenko: continue the offensive with 6th Army but send 23rd Tank Corps to defeat the German breakthrough. On the other side, Bock had far superior situational awareness than Timoshenko and, from his point of view, Kleist's rapid breakthrough meant that *Fridericus* had a real chance of pulling off a single envelopment of the Barvenkovo salient. He was concerned that VIII AK would collapse under the pounding of two Soviet tank corps, but ordered Paulus to transfer 3. and 23. Panzer-Divisionen as soon as possible to deal with the Soviet armour.

18 MAY

Due to poor communications and command indifference, Timoshenko's order to recall the 21st and 23rd Tank Corps was not implemented until 1200hrs. Gorodniansky finally had the bit between his teeth with VIII AK's front penetrated in two places and he was reluctant to surrender his trump card just because Kharitonov couldn't deal with Kleist on his own. Indeed, Soviet army-level commanders often cared little about what was going on in other sectors

and preferred that reinforcements come from either Front or Stavka reserves instead of their own resources. Consequently, Gorodniansky kept both tank corps in the line and the 23rd Tank Corps succeeded in capturing Karavan. Kuzmin's 21st Tank Corps spent most of the day inconclusively fighting the 113. Infanterie-Division around Borki and Ryabukhyne, losing 20 tanks in the process. Oberstleutnant Georg-Henning von Heydebreck's I/Pz.Rgt. 201 arrived to support the defence of Borki, which helped VIII AK to survive another day of hard pounding. Gorodniansky only allowed the 23rd Tank Corps to start moving east that evening, but it would not be in a position to contest Kleist's advance until the next day. He did not order the 21st Tank Corps to leave until the next morning. Thus initially, only the 2nd Cavalry Corps and the 343rd Rifle Division, both from Timoshenko's Front reserves, moved to reinforce 9th Army. Timoshenko asked the Stavka for more reinforcements but was told they would not arrive for at least three days. The lack of teamwork among Soviet senior leaders was a fatal weakness revealed in these critical days.

As the second day of *Fridericus* dawned, Kharitonov's 9th Army was already virtually *hors de combat*. The remnants of the 106th, 335th and 349th were encircled and bypassed east of Barvenkovo; Kleist committed the fresh 389. Infanterie-Division to crush this pocket, which it accomplished by the end of the day. While 1. Gebirgs-Division established a 'hard shoulder' west of Barvenkovo to thwart any move by 57th Army, the rest of Mackensen's corps pushed northwards, led by 14. Panzer-Division. Mackensen committed the 60. Infanterie-Division (mot.) to reinforce Kühn's advance. Hube's 16. Panzer-Division eviscerated Pliev's 5th Cavalry Corps, encircling part of it and scattering the remnants. Kharitonov's feeble effort to counterattack with the 15th and 121st Tank Brigades was completely ineffective. Incredibly, German troops reached Kharitonov's headquarters in Kamenka by 1000hrs and captured the southern part of Izyum by noon. The XXXXIV AK reached the Donets on a wide front after the remnants of 9th Army withdrew across the river, and Angelis deployed the 257. Infanterie-Division and 101. leichte Infanterie-Division to protect the right flank of the German breakthrough. The 97. leichte Infanterie-Division was positioned to capture the rest of Izyum, although the Soviet 343rd Rifle Division arrived in the northern part of the town that evening. By the end of the day, the 9th Army had no coherent front line, just pockets of individual resistance that fought without any coordination. The narrow neck of the Barvenkovo salient, now reduced to 30km, was only protected by remnants of Pliev's cavalry. Just before midnight, the 6th and 131st Tank Brigades from Pushkin's tank corps arrived near the neck after a

100km forced march. Perhaps the sole bright spot for the Soviets was that Podlas moved the 14th Guards Rifle Division and 2nd Cavalry Corps to build a new front facing east towards Barvenkovo; without this move, Mackensen would probably have rolled up 57th Army's flank forthwith.

19 MAY

Despite having stripped Gorodniansky of both tank corps, Timoshenko ordered 6th Army to continue advancing north towards Merefa and the west. In compensation, Timoshenko provided the fresh 103rd Rifle Division to Gorodniansky. He also ordered Bobkin, who had Krasnograd nearly encircled by Noskov's cavalry, to continue the offensive as well. The 6th Army now only had about 60–70 tanks left operational and limited stocks of artillery ammunition, but Gorodniansky continued probing attacks against VIII AK. However, the morning began badly when three KV-1 tanks stumbled into an ambush and were destroyed by 8.8cm Flak guns. Then Kampfgruppe Heydebreck (I/Pz.Regt. 201) counterattacked near Borki, overrunning Soviet infantry and an artillery battery. After losing 13 more tanks, the 41st Rifle Division and 49th Tank Brigade fell back, which indicated to Gorodniansky that real offensive action in his sector was no longer possible.

After securing the line of the Donets, Kleist spent the bulk of the day – unhindered by the Soviets – in resupplying his forces and concentrating the 14. and 16. Panzer-Divisionen and 60. Infanterie-Division (mot.) into a powerful mechanized assault group. With the remnants of the 9th Army sheltering behind the Donets, the only serious obstacle in Kleist's path was the blocking force near Grushevakha, consisting of two brigades of the 23rd Tank Corps and the battered 333rd and 341st Rifle Divisions. The 2nd Cavalry Corps and 14th Guards Division opposite 1. Gebirgs-Division were a lesser, but not inconsequential obstacle. Bock conferred with Hitler by telephone in the afternoon, who asked – not ordered – whether Kleist could advance any further. When Bock replied in the affirmative, Hitler authorized Kleist to advance north towards Protopopovka, one of the last Soviet-held crossing sites across the Donets and a vital link in 6th Army's lines of communication. Unlike Stalin's tight control over Timoshenko, Hitler did not interfere with Bock's battle command during the Kharkov campaign or even try to prevent units from retreating.

By mid-afternoon, Timoshenko finally accepted that he could not ignore Kleist's counteroffensive and that his own offensive would have to be suspended. At 1535hrs he telephoned Vasilevsky in Moscow and updated him on the situation. Vasilevsky had wanted to call off the offensive for two days but caved in to Stalin's demand to continue it. Timoshenko wanted permission to reorient the southern group and parts of Malinovsky's Southern Front to conduct a concentric attack against Kleist's assault group, thereby removing the threat to the salient. Vasilevsky hesitated because this course of action ran counter to Stalin's intent. After brief assurances that Timoshenko's forces could eliminate the German breakthrough in two to three days, Vasilevsky managed to convince Stalin to reorient the South-Western Front offensive and use its forces to crush Kleist's spearhead. After receiving Stalin's permission, Timoshenko issued a new series of orders to his scattered forces at 1720hrs. In a fit of sheer idiocy, he decided to scramble Bobkin's command and use its components to form an ad hoc grouping under his own deputy commander, General-Lieutenant Fedor I. Kostenko. Army Group Kostenko would comprise all of Bobkin's forces as well as three of Gorodniansky's rifle divisions and all the remaining tanks in the salient. Timoshenko ordered all forces facing westwards to shift to the defence and then issued an attack plan based on fantasy. Rather than massing forces against Kleist's spearhead in an effort to prevent the Germans from closing the trap, he ordered Kostenko to attack towards the north-east to capture Zmiev, cut through LI AK in the Balakleya salient and link up with a shock group from 38th Army. He ordered Podlas' 57th Army to try and envelop III AK (mot.) with the 2nd Cavalry Corps and 14th Guards Rifle Division, while the remnants of 9th Army were ordered to re-cross the Donets and attack the right flank of XXXXIV AK. Instead of a coordinated response, Timoshenko ensured that his last remaining combat power in the Barvenkovo salient was frittered away in piecemeal and divergent efforts.

20 MAY

During the night, Kleist transferred the 16. Panzer-Division efficiently from the centre of his spearhead over to his left flank to deal with the advance by the 2nd Cavalry Corps. Kleist intended to launch a surprise attack with Hube's Panzers, supported by 100. leichte Infanterie-Division and 1. Gebirgs-Division, in order to crush the 57th Army. Hube attacked at first light, inflicting heavy damage on the 2nd Cavalry Corps and advancing 30km. The five divisions of 57th Army were now threatened with being trapped in a mini-pocket south of Lozovaya and began thinning out their front line opposite the Romanians in order to create blocking forces east of Lozovaya. Although the attack gained considerable ground and smashed in the flank of 57th Army, it did not lead to the expected collapse, so Kleist decided to transfer Hube's Panzers back to his main drive to cut off the Barvenkovo salient. The rapid redeployment and attack by the 16. Panzer-Division was an amazing display of German tactical flexibility that caught the Soviets completely by surprise.

The rest of Mackensen's III AK (mot.) had continued advancing northwards, with 14. Panzer-Division pushing up the west bank of the Donets. Pushkin's 23rd Tank Corps had established a strong blocking around Mar'evka, but Kühn's Panzers simply skirted past it. Although the remnants of the 9th Army were on the defensive behind the Donets, the fresh 343rd Rifle Division succeeded in crossing the river and recapturing the southern part of Izyum, although that yielded no advantage. Malinovsky had also transferred one rifle division and tank brigade to replenish 9th Army and Timoshenko had another rifle division en route. Elsewhere, Army Group Kostenko began to disengage many of its forces, with 6th Cavalry Corps abandoning the siege of Krasnograd and the 21st Tank Corps belatedly moving towards Protopopovka. However, virtually all of the available Luftwaffe forces were pounding the Soviet forces inside the shrinking salient, disrupting communications and troop movements. Stukas from StG 77 succeeded in interdicting nine of the Donets River crossings, further isolating Soviet forces in the salient. Fuel and ammunition stocks were low before the Germans began capturing bridges over the Donets and were rapidly being exhausted.

21 MAY

Timoshenko was now gripped with a sense of urgency, realizing that the forces within the Barvenkovo salient were in dire peril. Inside the salient, Army Group Kostenko spent the majority of the day desperately trying to shift forces from the 6th Army area over to the Mar'evka region, but German air superiority and fuel shortages made this difficult. The only major addition to the Soviet forces defending the narrow neck was one brigade of the 21st Tank Corps. Outside the salient, Timoshenko formed another ad hoc formation known as Group Sherstiuk under General-Major Gavril I. Sherstiuk, the deputy commander of 38th Army. Sherstiuk took over the remnants of 9th Army and 5th Cavalry Corps, holding the eastern side of the Donets. Timoshenko's intent – which completely ignored the condition of his troops or available supplies – was that Kostenko and Sherstiuk would launch a coordinated attack against Kleist's spearhead around Petrovskaia within a day or two. He also pressured Moskalenko to attack the Chugeev salient to support Kostenko, but this was ignored.

Kleist had no intention of waiting around for either Timoshenko to reorganize his forces or for Paulus to get his Panzer divisions into action. Despite rain storms that interfered with Luftwaffe close air support, Mackensen had assembled the 14. and 16. Panzer-Divisionen plus the 60. Infanterie-Division (mot.) – a total of over 200 tanks and assault guns – around Petrovskaiga. Mackensen's attack ran into stiff resistance from the 23rd Tank Corps, costing him 21 tanks destroyed, but he managed to capture Mar'evka. Soviet tanks also tried to block the path to Protopopovka, but the 14. Panzer-Division fought its way through and occupied the town by dusk. Due to this advance, the neck of the Barvenkovo salient was narrowed to just 18km and Army Group Kostenko had its lines of communications reduced to a single bridge over the Donets at Ivanovka.

22 MAY

It was a hot day, with intermittent showers. Mackensen resumed his offensive after refuelling during the night. He put both Panzer divisions abreast and advanced due north, towards the AOK 6 stronghold at Balakleya. Kuzmin's 21st Tank Corps tried to block their path, but now had less than half its tanks and very little infantry support. After a series of tank actions,

LEFT
An SdKfz 250/3 radio half-track belonging to Armee-Gruppe von Kleist during *Fridericus*. These vehicles usually were assigned to the armoured infantry battalion in each Panzer division and they operated a number of radio nets, including for air-ground cooperation. (Bundesarchiv, Bild 169-0424)

RIGHT
A column of SdKfz 250 half-tracks passing an abandoned T-34 tank in the advance northwards. Increasingly, Soviet vehicles were abandoned for lack of fuel, as Army Group Kostenko's lines of communication were severed. (Ian Barter)

Mackensen's Panzers split the 21st Tank Corps into two pieces and continued north towards the Donets. As the Panzers neared the river late in the day, AOK 6's 44. Infanterie-Division sent an assault group across the river and linked up with Mackensen's vanguard. Army Group Kostenko was now isolated in the Barvenkovo pocket.

Adding to Timoshenko's problems, Paulus had managed to transfer the 3. Panzer-Division to Andreevka and it mounted a crossing operation over the Donets into the northern flank of 6th Army. Gorodniansky's infantry was caught flat-footed and the 337th Rifle Division was virtually encircled by nightfall. Group Sherstiuk tried to reopen a corridor to Kostenko by hurling the newly arrived 114th Tank Brigade with its American-made Grant and Stuart tanks into the flank of 14. Panzer-Division at Chepel, but Hube easily repulsed this pinprick. From past experience, the Germans knew that creating a pocket was relatively easy, but holding it closed was very difficult, so Kleist immediately moved to get infantry into the breakthrough corridor separating both Soviet groups. Accepting risk on the 57th Army front, Kleist pulled out the 1. Gebirgs-Division and sent it to reinforce Mackensen's Panzers. Consequently, the Italian Group Barbo and the four Romanian divisions were left holding more than a 100km stretch of front on their own. Yet the 57th Army was shifting most of its forces northwards and the Romanian 6th Corps even managed to advance about 5km into areas vacated by the retreating Soviets. With the Soviet offensive at an end, the battered VIII AK was able to stabilize its front and prepare to assist in the reduction of the pocket as well.

23 MAY

Kleist's primary objectives at this point were to widen the corridor between Kostenko's and Sherstiuk's forces and to reinforce the corridor with more infantry. The 16. Panzer-Division continued attacking towards the north-west and, by afternoon, linked up with Kampfgruppe Schmidt-Ott from 3. Panzer-Division near Glazunovka. As a by-product, the 337th Rifle Division was pinned against the Donets and encircled. Paulus also managed to bring up the 23. Panzer-Division and it would be ready to join the 3. Panzer-Division attack by the next morning. Meanwhile, German infantry was pouring into the corridor, first the 1. Gebirgs-Division and 384. Infanterie-Division, with more en route. During the day, the 57th Army evacuated Lozovaya and retreated north, which allowed the Romanians to advance and shorten their front, which enabled Kleist to shift the 100. leichte Infanterie-Division over.

Soviet efforts to break through the cordon proved weak and uncoordinated, serving only to consume their last stocks of fuel and ammunition. Kostenko conducted withdrawals in the west and south to concentrate his forces, but this only allowed the Germans to tighten the ring. Neither Group Sherstiuk nor the 38th Army could do much to help. Sherstiuk had only one rifle division and about 30–40 tanks. By the end of the day, Kleist had achieved his objective and widened the corridor to about 15km and built up a fairly solid bulwark on both sides. This was not Smolensk 1941, where Timoshenko had managed to salvage some of the encircled Soviet forces. Here, the Germans had rapidly and efficiently sealed the pocket and would soon begin reducing it. Soviet power was clearly fading on this battlefield and the prospects for a breakout or holding the pocket for an extended period were negligible.

THE END GAME, 24–29 MAY 1942

'Der ring um euch ist geschlossen!'

Report from III Armeekorps (mot.), 22 May

24 MAY

The Germans began the day with attacks around almost the entire perimeter of the Barvenkovo pocket. The most dangerous thrust was an attack by 3. and 23. Panzer-Divisionen, which expanded their bridgehead across the Donets and crushed the northern flank of 6th Army. Heitz's VIII AK increased the damage by attacking with the Hungarians and the 62. and 113. Infanterie-Divisionen, which advanced 13km and recaptured both Taranovka and Velikaya Bereka. The hapless 47th Rifle Division was shoved back 6–8km, losing most of the ground gained at great cost during 12–17 May.

The XI AK and 6th Romanian Corps attacked the western and southern sectors of the pocket, with the Romanians enjoying the most success. Timoshenko had stripped the 57th Army of resources back in April to provide forces for Army Group Bobkin and was now too weak and low on supplies to fend off attacks from south and east. In just two days, 57th Army retreated more than 50km back to Krasnopavlovka and 1,500 of its troops were captured. On the eastern side of the pocket, Mackensen steadily reduced the 23rd Tank Corps strongpoint near Federovka with Stuka attacks and artillery. Meanwhile, Group Sherstiuk sat immobile on the defence, waiting for reinforcements from 38th Army and Stavka reserves before resuming a relief effort.

German *Panzergrenadier* probe cautiously forwards during the *Kesselschlacht*. The trapped Soviet troops initially fought with great fanaticism and the Germans preferred to wear them down with airstrikes and artillery before closing in for the kill. (Ian Barter)

Note: Gridlines are shown at intervals of 5km/3.10miles

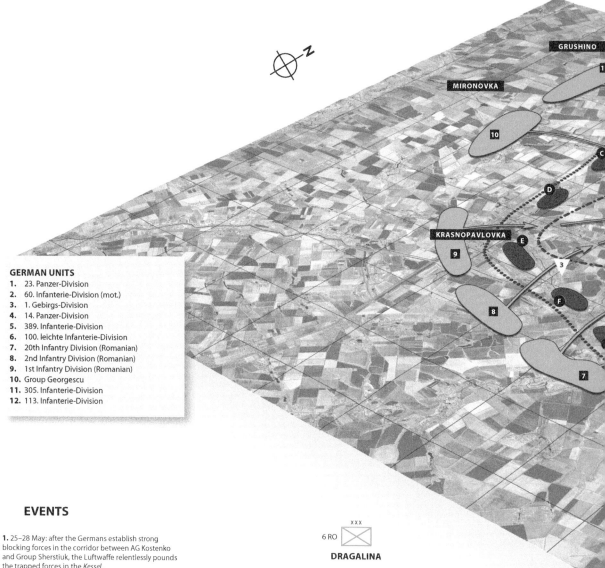

GERMAN UNITS

1. 23. Panzer-Division
2. 60. Infanterie-Division (mot.)
3. 1. Gebirgs-Division
4. 14. Panzer-Division
5. 389. Infanterie-Division
6. 100. leichte Infanterie-Division
7. 20th Infantry Division (Romanian)
8. 2nd Infantry Division (Romanian)
9. 1st Infantry Division (Romanian)
10. Group Georgescu
11. 305. Infanterie-Division
12. 113. Infanterie-Division

EVENTS

1. 25–28 May: after the Germans establish strong blocking forces in the corridor between AG Kostenko and Group Sherstiuk, the Luftwaffe relentlessly pounds the trapped forces in the *Kessel*.

2. 25 May: the 23. Panzer-Division attacks and pushes in the north-east corner of the *Kessel*.

3. 25 May: the Romanians and 100. leichte-Infanterie-Division rout the remnants of 57th Army and gain considerable ground.

4. 26 May: the 305. Infanterie-Division and Group Georgescu push in the western flank of the *Kessel*.

5. 26–28 May: repeated Soviet breakout efforts, with some survivors succeeding in slipping past the 60. Infanterie-Division (mot.).

6. 27–28 May: breakout efforts south of Lozovenka slip through first belt of German defences but are defeated by second belt.

7. 27 May: the Romanians and 305. Infanterie-Division begin rolling up the *Kessel* from the west and meet little resistance. By the end of the day, Romanians have linked up with Mackensen's III AK (mot.) on the Bereka.

8. 28 May: final Soviet resistance in the *Kessel* eliminated near Federovka.

6 RO XXX

DRAGALINA

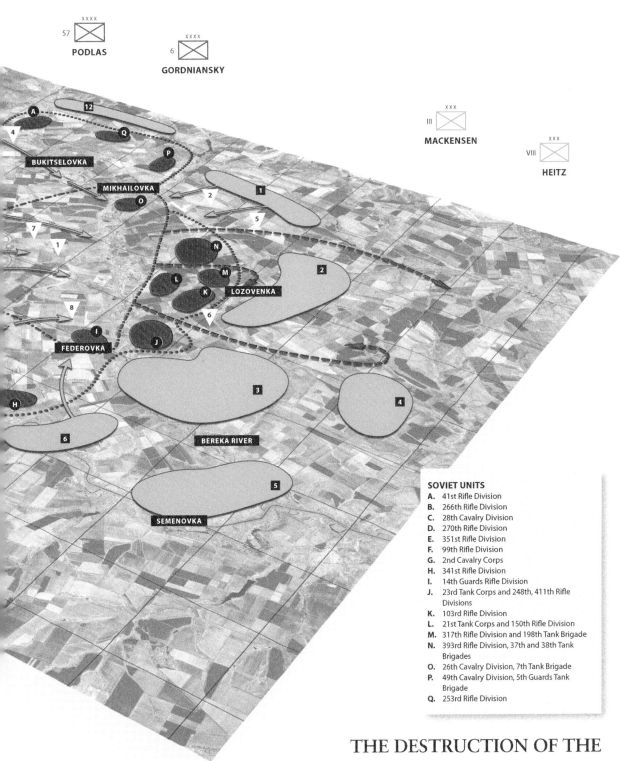

57 XXXX PODLAS

6 XXXX GORDNIANSKY

III XXX MACKENSEN

VIII XXX HEITZ

12

A
4
Q
P
BUKITSELOVKA
MIKHAILOVKA
O
7
1
2
5
1
N
2
M
L
K
LOZOVENKA
8
6
I
J
FEDEROVKA
H
3
4
6
BEREKA RIVER
5
SEMENOVKA

SOVIET UNITS
A. 41st Rifle Division
B. 266th Rifle Division
C. 28th Cavalry Division
D. 270th Rifle Division
E. 351st Rifle Division
F. 99th Rifle Division
G. 2nd Cavalry Corps
H. 341st Rifle Division
I. 14th Guards Rifle Division
J. 23rd Tank Corps and 248th, 411th Rifle Divisions
K. 103rd Rifle Division
L. 21st Tank Corps and 150th Rifle Division
M. 317th Rifle Division and 198th Tank Brigade
N. 393rd Rifle Division, 37th and 38th Tank Brigades
O. 26th Cavalry Division, 7th Tank Brigade
P. 49th Cavalry Division, 5th Guards Tank Brigade
Q. 253rd Rifle Division

THE DESTRUCTION OF THE BARVENKOVO *KESSEL*, 24–28 MAY 1942

The battered remnants of the Soviet 6th and 57th Armies are encircled in a *Kessel* around Federovka after Kleist's panzers have cut off the Barvenkovo salient. German and Romanian forces slowly crush the *Kessel* in a five-day battle, as the trapped Red Army units desperately try to break out to the east.

25 MAY

Army Group Kostenko began to fall apart, with command and control and supplies fading rapidly. In some sectors, units were retreating without orders or purpose. Groups of Soviet soldiers set off to the north, to the south, to the east, vainly looking for a way out of the trap. Caught in the open during daylight hours, the Luftwaffe rained down SD-2 anti-personnel bombs on them, slaughtering entire columns. Vehicles ran out of fuel and were shoved off the road, weapons ran out of ammunition and were abandoned. Eventually, the doomed procession veered eastwards towards their only hope – a breakout through the German cordon. Kostenko managed to assemble the bits and pieces of four divisions, perhaps 20,000–25,000 men, and flung them at the German cordon in a desperate effort to escape. Imbued with the courage of desperation, Kostenko's attack managed to gain some ground against the 60 Infanterie-Division (mot.) and reached the outskirts of Lozovaya. However, 1. Gebirgs-Division had already arrived in the corridor and it bloodily repulsed all Soviet efforts to break out.

Elsewhere, the 23. Panzer-Division managed to slice off the northern part of the pocket and isolate the 47th Rifle Division, while 3. and 16. Panzer-Divisionen smashed in the north-east corner of the pocket. The Romanians and the 100. leichte Infanterie-Division pushed the disorganized remnants of the 57th Army back as well. General-Lieutenant Podlas and his staff tried to break out to the east but were all killed or captured, leaving 57th Army without leadership. By nightfall, Kostenko had almost no combat-effective units left and the pocket was shrinking by the hour.

26 MAY

Army Group Kostenko continued to condense as the Axis cordon squeezed it from all sides. Bock himself came to observe as Kleist's forces relentlessly pounded the trapped Soviet forces with artillery and Stuka attacks, while Mackensen's infantry and Panzers steadily squeezed the pocket. By this point, Bock knew that *Fridericus* had succeeded completely and he was eager to give his forces time to rest and re-equip before Operation *Blau* began in late June. He directed Paulus to pull the 3. Panzer-Division out of the line to refit near Kharkov and recommended that Kleist avoid any unnecessary losses. Several more Soviet breakout attempts were foiled during the day and

A Soviet 122mm M1931/37 (A-198) gun abandoned, along with the American-built M3 Stuart light tank that was towing it. The M3 was probably assigned to the 114th Tank Brigade in Group Sherstiuk, which attempted to save some of the corps-level artillery regiments from the Barvenkovo *Kessel.* (Bundesarchiv, Bild 169-0423)

by evening the pocket had shrunk to only 15km across. During the day, General-Lieutenant Kostenko was killed leading one breakout effort and General-Major Bobkin was killed by German machine-gun fire. The Romanians and XI AK drove the fleeing Soviets towards Mackensen's Panzers, taking over 10,000 prisoners in one day.

27 MAY

The last remnants of Army Group Kostenko gathered in the valley of the Bereka River, where the road between Krutoiarka and Fedorovka became littered with the detritus of the vanquished Soviet armies. The best men and equipment available to the Red Army were now scattered across the flat terrain as if they were so much rubbish. Those units still with commanders and any remaining combat effectiveness made repeated efforts to break through the German cordon but were shot to pieces. General-Lieutenant Gorodniansky was killed in one of these final efforts. Some small groups succeeded in exfiltrating through the cordon and reaching Group Sherstiuk's position, but no organized units. The rest glumly awaited their fate in the pocket. Closing in, German infantry rounded up thousands more prisoners and then herded them up into long columns, which were driven westwards, where they would be beaten and starved into submission. It was a death march in all but name, without herald or post-war reunions. The only sour note for the Germans was an ugly fratricide incident when Stukas from StG 77 bombed infantry from II/Schützen-Regiment 126 (23. Panzer-Division) by mistake, killing 18 Germans and wounding 21 more.

THE ROAD OF DEATH, 26 MAY 1942 (PP. 84–85)

By the morning of 26 May, the remnants of Army Group Kostenko had been reduced to a pocket in the Bereka River valley that was approximately 20 x 20km. More than 200,000 troops and thousands of vehicles crowded along the road between Krutoiarka and Fedorovka, vainly trying to escape the pocket to the east. However, Kleist's forces had emplaced a very thick cordon around the pocket and the terrain was so open and flat that the Germans could easily detect every move. In order to conserve their ground units for subsequent operations, Bock ordered Kleist to rely upon artillery and air attacks to pulverize the trapped Soviet forces.

The Stukas of StG 77 **(1)** attacked repeatedly, striking any concentration of tanks, artillery or vehicles. Here, a Stuka is demolishing a battery of towed 122mm M30 howitzers on the road. Nearby, an He-111H level bomber **(2)** showers a Soviet infantry unit with SD-2 anti-personnel bombs, which were an early form of cluster munitions. German SC-250 bombs tossed T-34/76 tanks around like toys and smashed up lighter vehicles. Most of the Soviet vehicles were out of fuel and were now just sitting ducks. The dirt road and adjoining ravines soon became choked with wrecked vehicles and thousands of casualties **(3)**. German artillery added to the slaughter, bombarding the pocket continuously with long-range 10cm and 15cm rounds. Bock himself came to view the destruction of Army Group Kostenko, observing the operation from a hill near Lozovenka. A pall of smoke hung over the devastation, marking the death knell of Army Group Kostenko.

28 MAY

Organized resistance within the pocket ended, prompting Timoshenko to order all other forces in the South-Western and Southern Fronts to shift to the defence, in expectation that the Germans would attempt to press their advantage. During the night, General-Major Grigoriy I. Kuzmin led a final breakout effort by the remnants of his 21st Tank Corps and succeeded in bypassing German blocking units near Lozovaya. However, when the group encountered another German ambush near Volvenkovo, Kuzmin was badly wounded. Faced with the prospect of capture, he committed suicide.

29 MAY

Small groups of survivors trickled into Soviet lines near Chepel, one of which supposedly included six T-34 tanks. The Soviets later claimed that a total of 22,000 troops escaped the Barvenkovo pocket, but this is unlikely since all but a few units were disbanded after the battle. Very little of the cavalry within the pocket escaped, including General-Major Noskov, commander of 6th Cavalry Corps, who was captured by the Germans but managed to survive until the end of the war.

Two Soviet KV-1 heavy tanks and an elderly 76mm M1902/30 divisional gun lie abandoned in the *Kessel*. These tanks probably belonged to the 21st Tank Corps, which was destroyed near Lozovenka. (Ian Barter)

AFTERMATH

'An eye for an eye, a tooth for a tooth.'
Code of Hammurabi, 1792–1750 BC

Even by the standards of 1941, Timoshenko's South-Western Front had suffered a catastrophic defeat at Kharkov. All told, 16 rifle divisions, six cavalry divisions and four tank brigades were annihilated. Another dozen divisions were badly mauled and needed to be pulled out of the line for rebuilding. Of the 765,000 Soviet troops committed to the operation, a total of 277,190 became casualties – a 36 per cent loss rate. The Germans claim to have captured 239,000 prisoners. The three armies of the northern group suffered more than 54,400 casualties and the Southern Front's 9th and 57th Armies suffered 60,695 casualties. Yet perhaps the most shocking thing about the Kharkov debacle was the loss of vital command cadre. In contrast to other encircled Soviet armies in 1941–42, the collapse of the Barvenkovo pocket was so rapid that virtually no senior commanders escaped. The only significant survivor was General-Major Pushkin, who had the good fortune to be with part of his 23rd Tank Corps that was caught outside the pocket. Most of the division and brigade commanders were killed or captured, including Colonel Aleksandr I. Tavantsev, former commander of the 266th Rifle Division, who joined Vlasov's anti-communist army. As for the troops, the Germans were quick to recycle cooperative Soviet prisoners into use as auxiliaries known as *Hiwis* (helpers), while the remainder faced likely death in the POW camps.

After the *Kesselschlacht* ended, the Barvenkovo salient was littered with the debris of the shattered 6th and 57th Armies. Hundreds of wagons, trucks and tractors – smashed by artillery and air bombardment – were left to mark the last stand of many Soviet units. (Nik Cornish at Stavka)

The aftermath, June 1942

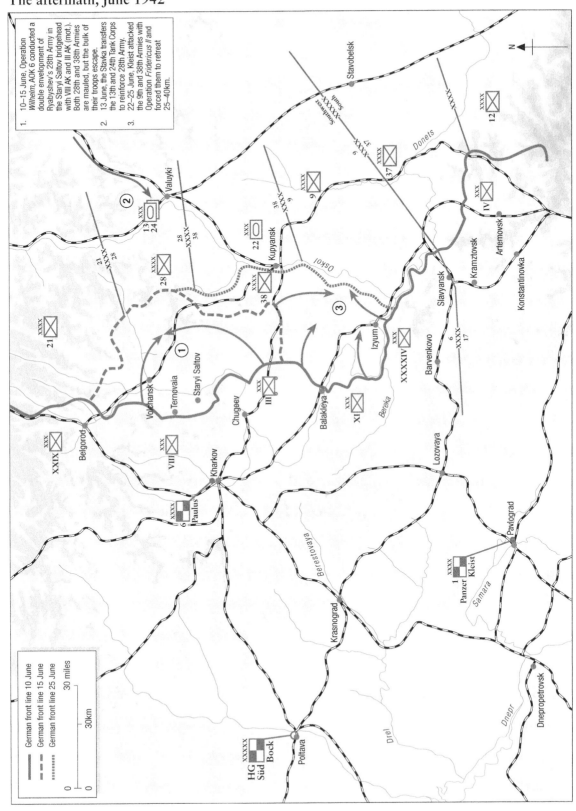

1. 10–15 June, Operation *Wilhelm*, AOK 6 conducted a double envelopment of Ryabyshev's 28th Army in the Staryi Saltov bridgehead with VIII AK and III AK (mot.). Both 28th and 38th Armies are mauled, but the bulk of their troops escape.
2. 13 June, the Stavka transfers the 13th and 24th Tank Corps to reinforce 28th Army.
3. 22–25 June, Kleist attacked the 9th and 38th Armies with Operation *Fridericus II* and forced them to retreat 25–40km.

German front line 10 June
German front line 15 June
German front line 25 June

0 ___ 30km
0 ___ 30 miles

Two abandoned BT-7 light tanks in a muddy field, somewhere in the northern sector. Although no major units in the northern group were encircled or destroyed, the offensive had cost it about two-thirds of its armoured strength. (Ian Barter)

In terms of material losses, the stockpile of equipment and supplies carefully gathered by the Stavka were squandered without accomplishing much. Out of the 1,200 Soviet tanks committed to battle around Kharkov, 775 were lost. One tank corps was completely destroyed and another rendered combat-ineffective. A total of 1,646 artillery pieces and 3,278 mortars were lost, including a great number of scarce 152mm howitzers. The VVS was completely outfought in the skies over Kharkov, losing 542 of 926 aircraft. Also significant, Timoshenko's forces lost over 57,000 horses in the operation, for which replacements could not simply roll off assembly lines.

After the debacle, there was a great deal of recrimination in the Kremlin about the defeat and its implications for the Soviet position on the southern part of the Eastern Front. General-Major Kharitonov was court-martialled for the rapid collapse of the 9th Army's defences, but once it became obvious how many mistakes were made at higher levels, the whole matter was dropped and Kharitonov was acquitted – an almost unheard of outcome in the Soviet system of military justice. Stalin was displeased with Timoshenko's dismal command performance but did not remove him immediately. Timoshenko remained in command of the South-Western Front when *Blau* opened on 28 June and then he was put in charge of the Stalingrad Front. Yet once it became clear that Timoshenko could not stop the inexorable German advance on Stalingrad, Stalin relieved him on 23 July.

Axis personnel losses during the Kharkov campaign were nearly 30,000, including at least 5,853 dead and 2,912 missing. Paulus' AOK 6 suffered 45 per cent of the total casualties, with its 294. and 62. Infanterie-Divisionen suffering 2,447 and 2,181 casualties respectively. The Romanians suffered 2,983 casualties, the Hungarians just 308 and the Italians less than 100. In material terms, German losses were quickly replaceable. The four Panzer divisions involved in the campaign lost 108 tanks out of 421 tanks committed – one quarter of their armour, but Germany built 325 medium tanks in May 1942 and could still replace these losses. Bock was more upset that AOK 6 lost a great deal of artillery during the campaign, often when batteries were overrun by Soviet tanks. The Luftwaffe lost about 91 of the 591 aircraft committed to the operation; 49 to enemy action and the rest to non-combat losses (including 35 fighters, 43 bombers and 13 ground attack).

A German mounted unit passes the wreck of an I-16 fighter on the Kharkov battlefield. Soviet air losses in the campaign were equally catastrophic and the Luftwaffe would enjoy air superiority in the southern part of the Eastern Front throughout the summer of 1942. (Ian Barter)

Both sides learned valuable, if not always correct lessons. The Germans learned that entrenched infantry and Flak guns could prevent Soviet armour from achieving a rapid breakthrough, buying time for Panzer reserves to arrive and rectify the situation. Based upon the performance of the Hungarians and Romanians in the battle, senior German leaders accepted the idea that they could be trusted to hold lengthy stretches of the front line – which would be proved wrong six months later. Vasilevsky and other thoughtful Soviet officers recognized that proper offensives required considerably more logistic preparation and staff coordination than had transpired in the South-Western Front. Likely German response actions also had to be considered in the planning process – not just wished away. Bloodied but wiser, the Red Army would take the lessons learned at great cost at Kharkov and incorporate them into Operation *Uranus* in November 1942.

The Germans captured over 200,000 Soviet prisoners during the *Kesselschlacht*. Note how few German guards were assigned to escort this long column. Many Soviet POWs volunteered to help the Germans as auxiliaries and AOK 6 marched on Stalingrad with over 50,000 of these men as *Hilfswilliger*. (Bundesarchiv, Bild 183-B26082, Fotograf: Schneider)

German *Panzerjäger* pull a 3.7cm Pak gun through an area littered with shell craters during one of the follow-up operations in June 1942. This time, German pincers failed to trap any large Soviet formations and AOK 6 was drawn further eastwards. (Ian Barter)

Bock only paused briefly to replenish his forces before pressing his advantage against Timoshenko's demoralized command. The elimination of the Barvenkovo salient greatly shortened his front line, allowing him to create reserves for the upcoming main event, *Blau*. As preliminaries to *Blau*, Paulus' AOK 6 conducted Operation *Wilhelm*, a double envelopment of Ryabyshev's 28th Army in the Staryi Saltov bridgehead on 10–15 June, which succeeded in capturing another 24,800 troops. On 22–25 June, Kleist attacked the 9th and 38th Armies with Operation *Fridericus II* and forced them to retreat 25–40km. Although Kleist failed to bag Moskalenko's 38th Army as intended, another 22,800 Soviet troops were captured. German losses in these battles totalled 7,486 casualties, including 1,573 dead or missing. Much of the Soviet equipment that survived the Kharkov offensive was lost during these two operations, including another 358 tanks and 376 artillery pieces, neither of which could be immediately replaced. When the main German summer offensive began on 28 June, the South-Western Front was too weakened to put up effective resistance. Retreat became the order of the day.

Formation	Dead	Wounded	Missing	Total
AOK 6	2,494	8,764	2,266	13,524
Armee-Gruppe von Kleist				
(III & XXXXIV AK)	1,836	5,771	234	7,841
XI AK	1,010	4,484	146	5,640
Romanian 6th Corps	513	2,204	266	2,983
TOTAL	5,853	21,223	2,912	29,988

Unit	Tanks declared 'total loss'			
	PzKpfw II	PzKpfw III	PzKpfw IV	Total
3. Panzer-Division	N/A	7	3	10
14. Panzer-Division	N/A	44	5	49
16. Panzer-Division	N/A	33	3	36
23. Panzer-Division	3	9	1	13
TOTAL	3	93	12	108

THE BATTLEFIELD TODAY

Today, Kharkov is now the second-largest city in an independent Ukraine. There are a number of English-speaking tour services available for battlefield visits in the region, as well as decent hotels and car rentals. The logical place to start to see things related to the 1942 Kharkov campaign is at the Kharkov Historical Museum, which has permanent displays on World War II. This display includes information on all three battles fought around the city in 1941–43 and the city's liberation in 1943. Like many museums in Eastern Europe, it is not open on Monday and has relatively short hours of access. There are also a number of significant World War II memorials around the city, including the Memorial to Guards Armoured Troops, the Liberation Memorial and the Cemetery of Honour and Memorial in the northern part of the city. With the fall of the Soviet Union, German veterans groups have had greater access to their former military cemeteries and there is now an immaculate German War Cemetery with about 40,000 graves north-east of the city. Lodging in the city is comfortable and transportation readily available, unlike some battlefields in the former Soviet Union.

Outside Kharkov, there are a number of Russian mass grave memorials in places such as Lozovenka and a memorial to Russian prisoners of war in Kirovograd. Izyum also has a number of memorials. Standard Soviet-era monuments, such as a T-34 tank or ZIS-3 field gun mounted on a plinth are still common sights throughout towns in the region. Yet most of the scenes of heavy fighting in May 1942, such as Ternovaya, are now just sleepy agricultural towns. Muddy, dirt roads and vast steppe land are still the norm, with few visible traces of a major campaign.

FURTHER READING

Primary records

Gefechtsbericht der 3. Panzer-Division (Kampfgruppe Breith) über die Abwehrschlact
        nordostwärts Charkow 12.5–22.5.42, NARA, T-315, Roll 144

Auszugsweiser Gefechtsbericht der 23. Panzer-Division für den Einsatz während der Schlacht
        um Charkow an der Nordfront vom 12.5–22.5, an der Südfront vom 23.5–29.5.42,
        NARA, T-315, Roll 791

Gefechtsbericht der 62. Inf. Div. über die kämpfe südl. Charkow in der Zeit vom 12-25.5.42,
        NARA, T-315, Roll 1034, frame 1225

Gefechtsbericht über den Einsatz in Krassnograd vom 14. – 22. 5.1942, NARA, T-312,
        Roll 1677, frames 653–62.

Various AOK 6 records, NARA, T-312, Rolls 1676–78.

Secondary sources

Bergstrom, Christer, *Black Cross – Red Star: The Air War over the Eastern Front,*
        Vol. 2 Pacifica, CA: Pacifica Military History, 2001

Gerbet, Klaus (ed.), *Generalfeldmarschall Fedor von Bock, The War Diary 1939-1945* Atglen,
        PA: Schiffer, PA, 1996

Glantz, David M. (ed.), *The South-west Front's Operations along the Khar'kov Axis in*
        May 1942 Self-published, 2006

Glantz, David M., *Kharkov 1942* Chatham, UK: Ian Allen, 1998

Hill, Alexander, 'The Allocation of Allied "Lend-Lease" Aid to the Soviet Union Arriving
        with Convoy PQ-12, March 1942 — a State Defense Committee Decree',
        The Journal of Slavic Military Studies, Vol. 19, Issue 4, 2006, pp. 727–38

Kissel, Hans, *Angriff einer Infanteridivision. Die 101. leichte Infanteriedivision in*
        der Frühjahrsschlacht bei Charkow Mai 1942 Heidelberg: Scharnhorst
        Buchkameradschaft, 1958

INDEX

References to illustrations are in **bold**